DEVOTIONS®

Dec. 2023–Feb. 2024

Without faith it is impossible to please God, because anyone who comes to him must believe that he exists and that he rewards those who earnestly seek him.

Hebrews 11:6

Christine Dallman, Editor

Photo © Getty Images

DEVOTIONS® Vol. 67, No. 1 is published quarterly by Standard Publishing, Colorado Springs, Colorado, www.standardpub.com. Copyright © 2023 by Standard Publishing, part of the David C Cook family, Colorado Springs, Colorado. All rights reserved. Topics based on the Home Daily Bible Readings, International Sunday School Lessons. Copyright © 2020 by the Committee on the Uniform Series. Printed in the U.S.A. All Scripture quotations, unless otherwise indicated, are taken from the Holy Bible, New International Version®, NIV® Copyright © 1973, 1978, 1984, 2011 by Biblica, Inc.® Used by permission. All rights reserved worldwide. Scripture quotations marked *(KJV)* are taken from the *King James Version*.

Faith That Pleases God

In the past there were times when, wanting to know if my faith was pleasing to God, I would begin looking at myself, wondering if I had the right amount of faith, or comparing my faith to someone else's, or thinking I was doing either pretty well or not so well in the faith department. But as time has passed, I've come to understand that faith that pleases God is not self-conscious in these ways.

God-honoring faith—rather than being mired in self-evaluation—is God-focused. You might even say it's God-enamored, insatiably interested in knowing who God is and what He is like. This kind of faith lives in wonder and delight at what God reveals of himself through His creation and in His Word. It is a faith that believes God truly exists, and it seeks—as a way of life—to know Him more and more.

Also, faith that pleases God is not about the amount of faith we can muster. Thankfully, it's not up to us to try conjuring "enough" faith but rather to just trust who God is. (In fact, if you think about it, faith in our own faith is a kind of idolatry.) So as we take that pressure off of ourselves, we can look to God and simply know and trust that anything is possible with Him (Genesis 18:14; Luke 1:37).

Yet faith that pleases God understands that God is not obligated to do things our way. While He *can* do anything, He will respond to our prayers from within His perfect wisdom, understanding, knowledge, goodness, timing, and purpose. And a God-pleasing faith steadies itself in what it knows of His faithful character, even when faced with confusion, disappointment, or even tragedy.

Finally, faith that pleases God does what is right and good and true as an outflow of reverence and love for Him. This kind of faith also shows mercy because gratitude for mercy received from God overflows in this way. And faith that pleases God walks humbly with Him, trusting Him so completely that whether God grants a petition right away, requires us to wait for His timing, or does something entirely different than what we'd hoped, we understand that God is not absent, cruel, unjust, inattentive, or indifferent, but that in His faithful love, He is working out everything for our good (Micah 6:8; Romans 8:28).

Peace to your heart!

Christine Dallman, Editor

December 1

Love Must Be Shared

He commanded us to preach to the people and to testify that he is the one whom God appointed as judge of the living and the dead (Acts 10:42).

Scripture: Acts 10:34-48
Song: "How Great Is Your Love"

Sharing with others doesn't come naturally to us. If we doubt this, we need only watch small children. Usually, they're not eager to let other children play with what's theirs. Occasionally, my two children shared voluntarily, but stinginess was the general rule. That's why parents must teach their children to share.

Peter struggled with stinginess too—stinginess with the gospel. He thought God gave the good news only to Jews like himself. To reveal the truth to Peter, God showed him a vision that helped Peter understand that the message of salvation was for *all* people. Then God sent Peter to a Gentile's house to share the gospel.

Ever since sin entered the world, prejudice and selfishness have plagued humanity. But God doesn't view us the way we often view each other. Regardless of where we've come from, God sees each of us as needing His loving redemption. And once we've recognized and received it, He wants us to share it freely, just as Peter did with the people gathered at Cornelius's house.

Father, as I have received Your saving love, help me be ready to share it with others today. In Jesus' name, amen.

December 1–3. **Martin Wiles** is a Christ-follower who is also a teacher, pastor, freelance editor, author, husband, father, and grandfather. He has authored seven books, and his work has been featured in numerous publications.

December 2

Reveling in Redemption

The women said to Naomi: "Praise be to the Lord, who this day has not left you without a guardian-redeemer" (Ruth 4:14).

Scripture: Ruth 4:13-22
Song: "Jesus Paid It All"

During my childhood, when my mom visited the local Piggly Wiggly grocery store, she received Greenbax stamps. The more groceries she bought, the more stamps they gave her. Also in town was a Greenbax store, where stamps could be redeemed for merchandise. Most of us are familiar with the idea of redeeming things like stamps and coupons for merchandise or discounts. The biblical idea of redemption, however, is the payment of a ransom to purchase back something that's been lost or forfeited—a rescue.

Ruth's predicament was dire: her husband had died, and now she lived (with her mother-in-law, Naomi) in a land foreign to her with no sustainable means of provision. However, Boaz was a relative who was eligible to purchase the land that belonged to Naomi's deceased husband. But if Boaz bought the land, he was obligated to marry Ruth, care for her needs, and have a family with her to carry on her late husband's name. In a beautiful picture of redemption, Boaz purchased the land and fulfilled his responsibilities to Ruth as a kinsman-redeemer.

Sinful humanity also finds itself in a predicament. But while we were still sinners, God sent Christ to pay our debt, providing redemption for all who will receive it. Once redeemed, our new life begins, and a new Heaven and new earth lie ahead!

Father, thank You for being my Redeemer who saves me from the penalty of sin and provides an eternal inheritance. In Jesus' name, amen.

December 3

Love Hangs On

Ruth replied [to Naomi], ". . . Where you go I will go, and where you stay I will stay. Your people will be my people and your God my God" (Ruth 1:16).

Scripture: Ruth 1:6-18, 22
Song: "Unending Love"

My paternal grandparents hung on through the good times and the lean times. Neither ever had a lucrative job, but they made ends meet, raised two children, cared for a nephew, and housed a parent. I recall my grandfather telling of how they once lived on $10 a week, but with that meager amount, they paid their bills and bought groceries. Just before my grandfather died, he and my grandmother both lay in a nursing home—in the same room and in twin beds pushed together so that they could hold hands.

The part of Ruth's story in today's passage is frequently used in marriage ceremonies to emphasize God's plan for marriages to endure and for the partners to be faithful. Ruth demonstrated her faithfulness by leaving her homeland and following her mother-in-law to a foreign land.

God's love for us hangs on. Once we are united with Christ by His saving grace, He promises never to leave or forsake us. He will hold our hand through the easy and challenging experiences. No matter how many times we may fail Him, when we return to Him, He will always receive us and offer a fresh start. And He wants us to return that dedication by loving Him with all our heart, soul, and mind (Matthew 22:37).

Father, help me to hold onto You tightly, as You hold onto me. In Jesus' name, amen.

December 4

God Leads the Way

[God said,] "As I was with Moses, so I will be with you; I will never leave you nor forsake you" (Joshua 1:5).

Scripture: Joshua 1:1-9
Song: "All the Way My Savior Leads Me"

When an exchange student arrived at our home, I showed her around: "Here are the light switches. . . . This is how to turn on the shower heater. . . . All your bath towels and soaps are in this closet." The young lady had traveled abroad before but never alone, and she needed detailed guidance in her new adventure.

After Moses died, God passed the baton of leadership to Joshua. Previously, when Joshua scouted the land of Canaan, Moses had been leading. But this time, Joshua was directly under God's leadership. So God assured Joshua that He would be with him and bring success as Joshua listened to and obeyed God.

It can be scary when God calls us to step into unfamiliar territory and do something new. But when He calls us, He also assures us that we don't need to be afraid. As we obey and follow His directions, He will bring about the success He has planned for us.

Father, thank You for giving me faith to follow You and for the clear instructions and assurance Your Word provides. In Jesus' name, amen.

December 4–10. **Rebecca Stuhlmiller** helps people take practical steps to grow deeper in their relationship with Jesus and wider in loving service to family, church, community, and the world in His name. She and her husband, Jeff, live in Federal Way, Washington.

December 5

Raise Your Hand

Two blind men were sitting by the roadside, and when they heard that Jesus was going by, they shouted, "Lord, Son of David, have mercy on us!" (Matthew 20:30).

Scripture: Matthew 20:25-34
Song: "Cry Out to Jesus"

In elementary school I got good grades and tutored classmates who struggled with their lessons. In secondary school I was promoted to accelerated classes, but I didn't feel smart anymore. I was afraid to raise my hand and embarrass myself, lest I ask a "dumb" question. But inevitably another student would pipe up and ask what I had been thinking, and I would kick myself for not speaking up.

As an adult, I sometimes hesitate to "raise my hand" in prayer. I've been told that God isn't a "genie in a bottle." *Don't ask a dumb question!* I second-guess my petitions in case my motives aren't pure. *Don't ask a dumb question!* But when Jesus passed by the blind men, they dared to speak up—even shout—and ask Him for what they wanted. I wonder how many people in the crowd, upon witnessing the verbal exchange and healing, wished they had been bold and spoken up too.

The men couldn't see Jesus with their eyes, but they saw Him with their hearts. He was the long-awaited Messiah, the one who had the power to give them what they needed. God knows what we need, and He welcomes our every request. He invites us to ask Him and then trust that He will answer according to His will.

Father, help me remember that You want me to boldly ask You for whatever I need. In Jesus' name, amen.

December 6

Yes, and Amen

[Jesus said,] "If you believe, you will receive whatever you ask for in prayer" (Matthew 21:22).

Scripture: Matthew 21:18-22
Song: "Breakthrough"

Darin's parents and some Bible school students went to visit a man who was near death at a hospital in the African country of Burundi. The doctor asked the group not to visit because the man was too weak. Right away, the students began praying for the man's healing. One said, "If anyone doesn't believe God can heal this man, they should leave the room now." Darin's dad began praying the prayer of the father in Mark 9:24—"I do believe; help me overcome my unbelief!"—and the dying man was healed completely.

Years later, Darin prayed for his dad's complete healing from cancer, but instead of being healed, his father passed away a few weeks later. Darin testifies, "I know God can heal, but I also know sometimes He chooses not to do so."

In my own life, I experienced something similar when my brother was in a motorcycle accident and suffered a traumatic brain injury. I believed for a miraculous healing, but my brother died 18 days later. Maybe you're praying for healing or for a different kind of "mountain to move" in your life. Perhaps you're imagining what God's best answer would look like to you; but Scripture reminds us that while we only need to have faith as small as a mustard seed (Matthew 17:20), God's ways are not our ways (Isaiah 55:8-9). We must pray, believe, and then trust in His wisdom.

Father, thank You that You're worthy of my trust and You answer each prayer. In Jesus' name, amen.

December 7

By Our Side

The LORD is my light and my salvation—whom shall I fear? The LORD is the stronghold of my life—of whom shall I be afraid? (Psalm 27:1).

Scripture: Psalm 27
Song: "A Mighty Fortress Is Our God"

Although I attended public high school, our varsity choir closed every concert by singing Martin Luther's hymn "A Mighty Fortress Is Our God." But even for me, a regular churchgoer, the message of the powerful song went in one ear and out the other. I sang the words by rote, mechanically, without thinking of their meaning. I might as well have been singing a nursery rhyme.

Later in my young-adult life, when I was struggling with trials and feeling overwhelmed, the lyrics of the oft-sung hymn would pop into my head, and the second verse especially comforted me: "Did we in our own strength confide, / Our striving would be losing; / Were not the right Man on our side, / The Man of God's own choosing: / Dost ask who that may be? / Christ Jesus, it is He; / Lord Sabaoth, His Name, / From age to age the same, / And He must win the battle."

King David faced intense battles and poured out his problems in the Psalms, but he also acknowledged that he was not alone. God was with him and fighting for him. In the same way, when we feel overloaded, we can read the Bible, meditate on its truth, and be assured of God's presence, protection, and power—no matter what we are facing.

Father, thank You for being a mighty fortress and my helper. I praise You that no one on earth is Your equal. In Jesus' name, amen.

December 8

In Line with Scripture

What you heard from me, keep as the pattern of sound teaching, with faith and love in Christ Jesus (2 Timothy 1:13).

Scripture: 2 Timothy 1:3-14
Song: "How Firm a Foundation"

I once hired a professional to hang wallpaper in my kitchen. As I watched the woman work, I learned about the plumb line, a cord covered with chalk with a weight at the end. When the cord was snapped against the wall, the chalk left a vertical line that served as a guideline to hang the next strip of paper. Without a plumb line, the designer would have to eyeball it and decide what looked straight. The first strip of paper she laid might be close, but it wouldn't be perfect. After hanging a few strips, the paper would end up crooked, and the project would be a mess.

A similar thing can happen in our own lives if we read the truth in God's Word, then rely on our own understanding. We might begin with right perspective, but we hear a sermon or read an article based on a person's opinion, and one decision at a time, we veer off-course and find ourselves unaligned with God's precepts.

Just as a designer uses a plumb line to keep on track, we must consistently measure what we hear against God's plumb line—His Word. Otherwise, we can move far away from God and what is right, not realizing where we went wrong.

Father, thank You for giving me Your Word as a "plumb line" by which I can always measure my thoughts and actions. In Jesus' name, amen.

December 9

Underlying Issues

Eliab, David's oldest brother, . . . burned with anger at [David] and asked, "Why have you come down here? And with whom did you leave those few sheep in the wilderness?" (1 Samuel 17:28).

Scripture: 1 Samuel 17:1, 3-4, 8, 20-30
Song: "Voice of Truth"

When the Pacific Northwest clouds don't obscure the view and "the mountain is out," I stand in awe of the magnificent, snowcapped Mount Rainier. But as a resident of the surrounding community, I also know that Mount Rainier is a seething, active volcano. Beneath the breathtaking surface lies a smoldering magma chamber that one day may blow, burying the region in lava and ash.

Jesse told David to deliver supplies and check on his brothers, and when David arrived at the battlefield, he dutifully carried out his father's business. But when he heard Goliath's taunts, his attention turned toward his Heavenly Father's business. Everyone wanted the Philistines to be defeated, but no one except the young shepherd stepped forward. At David's interest in the situation, Eliab erupted in anger, his sarcastic reaction revealing a smoldering resentment toward his younger sibling.

Jesus told the Pharisees that "the mouth speaks what the heart is full of" (Matthew 12:34). Sometimes people we know and love blow up and spew hurtful words based on emotions that have been seething beneath the surface. As followers of Jesus, filled with the Holy Spirit, we can check our initial reaction and ask God to help us respond with grace and truth.

Father, help me take a step back when I'm the recipient of hurtful words and respond with Your patient wisdom. In Jesus' name, amen.

December 10

Start with *Why*

[David said,] "I come against you in the name of the LORD Almighty, the God of the armies of Israel, whom you have defied" (1 Samuel 17:45).

Scripture: 1 Samuel 17:31-37, 45, 48-50
Song: "My Tribute"

In his *TED Talk* "How Great Leaders Inspire Action," Simon Sinek draws a target of three concentric circles. In the outer circle he writes the word *What;* in the second circle, *How,* and inside the bull's-eye, *Why.* Most people striving for success start with *what* they should do, Sinek says. Next, they decide *how* they should do it. However, there's not much thought given to *why.* He clarifies that making money is a result, not a reason, and often, the attempt to succeed fails because the approach is backward. Sinek asserts that successful people and businesses first start with *why,* a core belief or conviction.

The shepherd boy David was not yet a king, but he had been anointed by God. When he heard Goliath's threat against God and His people, David knew *what* to do: combat this enemy. David knew *how* to do it: with his slingshot. But ultimately David's motivation was found within *why* he needed to do it: to defend God's great name.

As followers of Jesus who are serving in His kingdom, we know *what* to do: make disciples of Jesus. With God's direction, we learn *how* to do it, using the skills and gifts with which we've been equipped. But *why* we do it will be the lasting motivation: we do all things for the glory of God.

Father, living to glorify You is my greatest motivation. In Jesus' name, amen.

December 11

Busted!

As [Tamar] was being brought out, she sent a message to her father-in-law. . . . "See if you recognize whose seal and cord and staff these are" (Genesis 38:25).

Scripture: Genesis 38:6-11, 13-18, 24-26
Song: "Great Are You Lord"

Scenic back roads beckon me home each day after work. It's a relaxing drive following a long day. Spotting deer or a flock of turkeys is common, but it can also be easy to speed. Recently, I popped over a hill, and a police car sat beside the road with a radar gun pointed my way. I hit my brakes too late. He pulled out behind me and threw on his lights. Busted! Slowly, I pulled over and awaited punishment. Thankfully, the officer met me with sweet mercy and gave me a warning instead of a ticket.

When we're not keeping in step with God's Spirit, we end up on the wrong side of God's law of love. Our flesh is rebellious, selfish, desiring its own way instead of the good things God has planned for us. When we confess our sin, however, God meets us with mercy, just as He did when we first came to Him for salvation.

In God's great plan, Jesus took our sin on himself so that we could be free to live in fellowship with Him and learn to walk in His ways. In Him, we go from busted to beloved.

Father, thank You for extending Your sweet mercy. I'll honor You by extending mercy to others. In Jesus' name, amen.

December 11–17. **Melinda Eye Cooper** lives in Tennessee. She has three sons, two daughters-in-law, four beautiful granddaughters, and a spunky dog.

December 12

Little Signs

[Rahab said,] "Give me a sure sign that you will spare the lives of my father and mother, my brothers and sisters, and all who belong to them—and that you will save us from death" (Joshua 2:12-13).

Scripture: Joshua 2:1-6, 8-16
Song: "Himself"

When a new job came my way with a company that managed homeowner associations, it was a refreshing change. But I knew nothing about the business. Once I started to learn my new job, I began noticing little signs staked in the ground outside of many subdivisions, each one indicating who managed the property. Due to all I'd learned, I now knew what they meant, and I saw them everywhere.

Rahab was outside Israel's community, and so she understandably sought a sure sign to guarantee the safety of her family. In our own lives as believers, we may be tempted to seek a sign from God for assurance or to help us find His direction.

However, as God's people, instead of looking for a sign from God, we can seek God himself. In our genuine search to draw near to Him, we'll come to know Him increasingly and find Him faithful. Then we'll see the many signs of His protection and provision in our lives that, perhaps, we'd been overlooking because we didn't really know Him well enough. Through studying His Word, praying full-heartedly, and surrendering our will to His, we'll see signs of His goodness everywhere. When we're seeking Him in these ways, He won't fail to reveal His love to us.

Father, I don't need signs because I know I can trust You. In Jesus' name, amen.

December 13

The Trust Test

As you know, we count as blessed those who have persevered. You have heard of Job's perseverance and have seen what the Lord finally brought about. The Lord is full of compassion and mercy (James 5:11).

Scripture: James 5:1-11
Song: "Walk by Faith"

Money was tight when my kids were young. Once, I put $10 worth of gas in my car and handed a check to the cashier. She handed me back $90 in cash. I held the money, confused for a moment, and then realized the problem. "My check was for $10," I said as I handed back the cash. She put the money in her cash drawer, and I headed to my car with a heavy heart. I *needed* $90. Doing the right thing doesn't always feel good.

Job persevered during God's thorough examination of his faith. At the end of that testing, God brought tremendous blessing. God will also test us. When He does, it may be that He's building our faith or teaching us an important lesson. Sometimes the testing may be brief, or it may take years.

God gives the most important and vital tests. He knows us inside and out. He knows our thoughts, intentions, and attitudes (Psalm 139:1-4). He finishes the work He has begun in us to make us more like Jesus (Philippians 1:6). We can expect a trust test or two along the way, but we can also know that God keeps His promises and is forever faithful.

Father, help me persevere during times of trial, knowing You are establishing my trust in You. In Jesus' name, amen.

December 14

Forgotten Spanking

Even though I was once a blasphemer and a persecutor and a violent man, I was shown mercy because I acted in ignorance and unbelief (1 Timothy 1:13).

Scripture: 1 Timothy 1:12-17
Song: "Grace Greater Than Our Sin"

One Sunday when I was a kid, I was behaving badly in church. After multiple warnings from my dad to "straighten up," he resorted to promising me a spanking when we got home. His words finally forced me to behave. The time seemed to creep slowly by as we drove home from church, and my angst grew with each passing mile. When we got home, I went straight to my room and stayed there, and before I knew it, bedtime came. I slipped peacefully to sleep, thankful for my dad's forgetfulness.

Paul knew how badly he'd behaved before his life-changing encounter with Jesus. He was grateful for God's mercy toward him. Our Heavenly Father has been merciful toward us as well, giving us what we don't deserve (mercy) and withholding from us what we do (punishment). He lavishes kindness on us by giving us an abundant life through His Son, including eternal life with Him in Heaven.

My dad probably didn't forget my bad behavior and his promise to spank me. He just chose to extend grace and mercy. God deals with us as His children in a similar way. He is gracious toward us and full of mercy. There is no greater parent, and He loves us more than we can imagine.

Father, thank You for Your incredible mercy and forgiveness. I will live gratefully today in Your love. In Jesus' name, amen.

December 15

The Greater Good

David pleaded with God for the child. He fasted and spent the nights lying in sackcloth on the ground (2 Samuel 12:16).

Scripture: 2 Samuel 11:1-5, 26–12:1-8, 15-18, 24
Song: "Even If"

My co-worker Christi broke the fibula in her lower left leg while playing miniature golf. She had surgery to repair the bone, and the surgeon put a metal plate in her leg. Part of her recovery included physical therapy twice a week. We were discussing her therapy one day, and she said, "It's painful to endure, but it will be worth it to heal properly. It's for the greater good." Her words were about her body, but they resonated with spiritual truth.

David did everything within his power to save his child, but it didn't change the outcome. Accepting God's will for our lives can be tough, and keeping our hearts from hardening can be a challenge. We can't see the greater good when our vision is blurred with tears. But God sees the big picture and is working everything for our good—even the hardest things to understand.

We need to heal properly after a trauma in life. Even in healing, though, there will be pain. We may grieve deeply, but grief is part of healing. Placing our trust in God's sovereign plan, as David did, is an important part of healing properly. In life, we might do everything within our power to help our situation, but ultimately, we need to trust God's wisdom.

Father, even in my pain, help me trust Your wisdom and goodness. In Jesus' name, amen.

December 16

Why Don't You Trust Me?

Those who know your name trust in you, for you, Lord, have never forsaken those who seek you (Psalm 9:10).

Scripture: Psalm 9:1-14
Song: "'Tis So Sweet to Trust in Jesus"

Why don't you trust Me with your children? It seemed God was speaking clearly to my spirit, and it stunned me as I wrestled with the idea of putting my 3-year-old in childcare. I didn't realize that by worrying about my youngest son's care, I wasn't trusting God. I didn't want him in childcare, but I knew I needed to work. Immediately, I placed my trust in God and began a local job search. I left childcare in God's powerful hands. Amazingly, I ended up with a job at a church with *free* onsite childcare.

Incredible things happen when we trust the one who loves us most. Trusting Him through one life experience after another underscores the truth of His Word: He is trustworthy. If things go well, we can praise Him. If things go sideways, we can look to Him prayerfully to lead us through the difficult times. Eventually, the outcome of our trust in Him will manifest as unshakable faith. In fact, our trials build trust in a way nothing else can.

Trusting God in those hard places where we must let go of our desires leads us into a relationship with Him that is deeper than we could have otherwise known. He already knows our thoughts, fears, and intentions. He works for our good and always has our best interests at heart in any and every situation.

Father, show me areas in my life where I need to trust You more. In Jesus' name, amen.

December 17

Make Jesus Known!

Salmon the father of Boaz, whose mother was Rahab, Boaz the father of Obed, whose mother was Ruth, Obed the father of Jesse, and Jesse the father of King David. David was the father of Solomon, whose mother had been Uriah's wife (Matthew 1:5-6).

Scripture: Matthew 1:1-17
Song: "Only Jesus"

During rush hour at a Washington, D.C., subway, a well-known violinist played anonymously, not for attention but as an experiment. In 43 minutes, Joshua Bell played six classical masterpieces on one of the most expensive instruments in the world. A total of 1,097 people passed by as he played. Few stopped to listen. They didn't know that the person playing in the subway had sold out a symphony hall only three days earlier. In fact, only one person recognized him.

In today's passage, Bathsheba is mentioned only as Uriah's wife, even though she was the mother of Solomon, one of history's most famous kings. It's a reminder that while we may wish to be seen and acknowledged for who we are and what we have accomplished, at times we might not be. Of course, that can be frustrating because, by nature, we want to be known and to make our mark on the world.

But truth be told, the real name worth knowing and making known is *Jesus.* People all around us need to know of Him and His gift of salvation. God offers the "music" of His beautiful gospel, and He sends it to places we might never expect to go. Let's follow Him there!

Father, grant me courage to speak the gospel boldly and to make Your Son's name known. In Jesus' name, amen.

December 18

Keeping Up

I have learned the secret of being content in any and every situation, whether well fed or hungry, whether living in plenty or in want (Philippians 4:12).

Scripture: Philippians 4:10-19
Song: "Enough"

Some people finished their gift shopping months ago, while others will wait until Christmas Eve to even begin. Likely a few folks are panicking today, thinking that they haven't bought enough—or at least not enough to keep up with everyone else. They're stressed by the idea of another family buying something for their children that is significantly more exciting than what they were able to buy or maybe more than what they can reciprocate.

This perspective puts too much emphasis on the riches of this world instead of on the provisions and blessings of God. While there's nothing wrong with generous giving at Christmastime, being content with the blessings of health and family is just as important. Today's passage reminds us that Paul had learned to be content in any and all circumstances.

Maybe you're feeling stressed by the pressure the culture puts on us during this season. Let's slow down and take inventory of the ways God has blessed us and be satisfied with what we have and are able to give.

Father, as the days approach to celebrate Christmas, I'll be content with how You have blessed me and with what I am realistically able to give others. In Jesus' name, amen.

December 18–24. **Mark Williams** is a pastor, college professor, and freelance writer who lives with his wife and children near York, Pennsylvania.

December 19

Coming to the Rescue

"Because he loves me," says the LORD, "I will rescue him; I will protect him, for he acknowledges my name" (Psalm 91:14).

Scripture: Psalm 91:1-16
Song: "Rescue the Perishing"

Many of the most beloved fairy tales involve a heroine being rescued from an evil villain by a tall, dark, and handsome hero. The power of the story comes from the victory of good over evil. Whether being rescued from a tower, an evil stepmother, or some other menace, the plot always plays out the same, with the hero and heroine riding off into the sunset together and living "happily ever after."

Two thousand years ago, God's people were walking in darkness, imprisoned by their own brokenness and sin. The psalmist envisioned a time when God would come to their rescue, and this rescue did finally come in the form of the baby Jesus, born in a stable in a small town in the remote countryside. Jesus would walk the road from the cradle to the cross to bring life to those who would trust in Him.

As we prepare to celebrate next week with our family and friends, it could be easy to forget that the Christmas story is truly a rescue story. May our hearts be filled with the joy of knowing that God loves us beyond our comprehension and that He sent Jesus to rescue us and give us eternal life!

Father, thank You for coming to my rescue—for bringing me out of the darkness and into Your light. I praise You for providing this gift of abundant life! In Jesus' name, amen.

Fortunes Restored

[God said,] "I will repay you for the years the locusts have eaten—the great locust and the young locust, the other locusts and the locust swarm—my great army that I sent among you" (Joel 2:25).

Scripture: Joel 2:18-27
Song: "Greater"

For more than 100 years, Kodak was the most recognizable name in photography. However, in the late 1990s, digital photography came on the scene, and Kodak speculated that it was only a passing fad. This proved to be an unfortunate miscalculation that led to the company filing for bankruptcy in January of 2012. Though this could have been the end for Kodak, the company rebounded and resurfaced as a technology company focused on imaging. In 2021, the company boasted a net income of $24 million.

In today's passage the prophet tells of a time when the land of Judah would become bankrupt from an intense season of drought and famine. There would be much loss and suffering but, in time, through the Lord's mercy, the fortunes of the people would be restored. Though what was lost could not be regained, God would give them hope for the days to come.

Still today, God's people often make mistakes that cost them decades of joy and peace. Many feel their sinful choices have disqualified them from God's grace and that there is no hope for restoration. The Christmas season reminds us that God sent Jesus to earth to bring salvation and restoration to *all* who will receive Him.

Father, remind me today that Your grace is greater than all my sins, failures, and mistakes. In Jesus' name, amen.

December 21

Coming Home

[The angel said,] "He [John] will bring back many of the people of Israel to the Lord their God" (Luke 1:16).

Scripture: Luke 1:5-17
Song: "The Heart of Worship"

When I was growing up, children knew the sound of their mother's voice or whistle as the call to come and "wash up" for dinner. After hours of playing out in the summer sun, when that call came, bare feet went pounding down the sidewalk. You didn't want to be late getting home!

In the time of Zechariah, God had been silent for more than 400 years, and His people had wandered far from His path. In His infinite wisdom, God knew it was time to intercede in His creation once again. As a prelude to the birth and ministry of Jesus, God would send Zechariah's son, John, to bring a message of repentance, calling God's people back to righteousness. John would come in the spirit of the prophet Elijah, breaking the silence with a new message of God's love for His people.

In the same way that we knew and listened to our mother's voice as children, we can learn to hear and know the voice of God as well. As we walk closely with God through the years, we learn to sense when we are wandering from His path and can discern His call to come home to "wash up" and return to walking with Him.

Father, I don't want to delay getting back home to Your will and Your ways. I will respond right now to Your call to return to You. In Jesus' name, amen.

December 22

Imposed Silence

The angel said to [Zechariah], "I am Gabriel. I stand in the presence of God, and I have been sent to speak to you and to tell you this good news. Now you will be silent and not able to speak until the day this happens, because you did not believe my words, which will come true at their appointed time" (Luke 1:19-20).

Scripture: Luke 1:18-25
Song: "Word of God, Speak"

In today's busy way of life, times of silence have become quite rare. From the moment the alarm goes off, some folks try to fill every minute with sound, including turning on "white noise" at night to help them sleep. As a result, most people are never alone with their own thoughts.

This was not the case for the priest Zechariah after he was visited by an angel of God. Because he hesitated to believe what the angel told him, his ability to speak was taken away. This gave Zechariah plenty of time to contemplate God's power and to reflect on God's desire to answer the prayers of those who faithfully serve Him.

In a world of busyness and noise, it is vital that we find time when we can be alone in God's presence to read His Word, to reflect on His commands and promises, and to respond in the strength of His Holy Spirit. By shutting out the noise of our electronic devices and their demands on our time and attention, we can set aside space to be still before God.

Father, today as I spend quiet moments in Your presence, may my heart receive and believe Your Word. In Jesus' name, amen.

December 23

Without a Doubt

Then [Jesus] said to Thomas, "Put your finger here; see my hands. Reach out your hand and put it into my side. Stop doubting and believe" (John 20:27).

Scripture: John 20:19, 24-29
Song: "Only Believe"

Most North American children grow up believing in Santa Claus as the great giver of Christmas gifts—that is, until they grow older and begin suspecting that Santa's work is in fact their parents buying gifts for them. Doubts usually start when a friend or sibling boldly declares that Santa doesn't exist or when the child finds Christmas gifts hidden in a closet. Eventually, the whole myth falls apart under the weight of mounting evidence against Santa's existence.

While many of the other disciples had seen the resurrected Jesus with their own eyes, Thomas had not yet. The grieving disciple needed clear evidence before he'd be willing to believe Jesus was alive. Unless Thomas could see the risen Jesus for himself, he refused to believe. When Jesus came into the Upper Room, He gave Thomas definitive proof that He was indeed alive, risen from the grave.

It is easier to doubt than to believe what you can't see; such believing requires faith. Thomas eventually responded in faith because he could see and touch Jesus. But even though we cannot touch the scars of Jesus, we can have faith that His love for us is real and His sacrifice will bring us life!

Father, today help me believe in You and not doubt. Strengthen my faith in Your Word and in Your unfailing love for Your people. In Jesus' name, amen.

December 24

Never Alone

[The angel told Mary,] "Even Elizabeth your relative is going to have a child in her old age, and she who was said to be unable to conceive is in her sixth month" (Luke 1:36).

Scripture: Luke 1:36-45, 56
Song: "Away in a Manger"

Expecting a baby can be one of the most exciting and stressful seasons in life. It sets in motion months of planning and dreaming, complete with big announcements and joyous months of preparation. The crib must be purchased and put together, car seats have to be acquired and installed, and the nursery needs to be painted and decorated. Along the way, hopefully there will be lots of support from family and friends.

When the angel appeared to Mary, he told her the shocking news that, even though she was a virgin, she would become pregnant with the coming Messiah. This pregnancy would happen when the Holy Spirit "overshadowed" her (Luke 1:35). Mary was overwhelmed and perhaps felt scared and alone. The angel encouraged her by revealing that Mary's relative Elizabeth was also miraculously pregnant in her old age. Mary hurried to be with Elizabeth, and together they carried the joy and uncertainty of what was to come.

In this Christmas season, we may be facing times of uncertainty and fear, but we don't have to walk through these times alone. Even when we think no one else understands, we can find strength in God's presence and in our relationships with those closest to us.

Father, thank You that in my times of need Your presence surrounds me, and Your people uplift me. In Jesus' name, amen.

December 25

Steps of Faith

When Joseph woke up, he did what the angel of the Lord had commanded him and took Mary home as his wife (Matthew 1:24).

Scripture: Matthew 1:18-25
Song: "Joseph's Song"

A 24-year-old woman felt like she had a scarlet letter on her forehead. Coming out of a world of abuse, she couldn't imagine anyone wanting to be with her. Then it happened. A Christian man set his eyes on her and refused to let her past dictate his perspective. He married her and showed her how God's love could help heal the pain of the past.

Mary was likely even younger than that woman when Mary learned she was to be a pregnant bride. Did she wonder whether Joseph would refuse to marry her? After all, marrying her was a risk. People would talk. However, Joseph was a man who honored God, and in doing so, he honored Mary, the one who would give birth to God's Son.

When we begin to do something for God's kingdom that feels risky, we might fear what could happen. But Proverbs 3:5 instructs us to trust in the Lord wholeheartedly. We can give Him the sacrifice of our obedience today as we step out in faith and see what He will do.

Father, thank You for the gift of Your presence and Your guidance in my life. Grant me courage to risk greatly for Your kingdom. In Jesus' name, amen.

December 25–31. **Jennifer Turner** lives in the Charlotte, North Carolina, area with her husband and three children. She enjoys speaking and writing about the goodness of God, His abundant grace, and His redemptive love.

December 26

Hunger for Him

[Mary said,] "He has filled the hungry with good things but has sent the rich away empty" (Luke 1:53).

Scripture: Luke 1:46-55
Song: "We Hunger and Thirst"

"It's a miracle!" I exclaimed one afternoon. I was 5 years old, and that morning my family and I had prayed a bold prayer of faith. With bare cabinets and an empty refrigerator, we had nothing to eat for lunch or dinner that day. So we prayed for what we needed, went to church, and came home to bags of groceries on our doorstep.

This story of God's provision easily comes to mind when I read Mary's words of praise about God filling the hungry with good things. The part that might be hard to understand, though, is that God sends the rich away empty. But Mary isn't just talking about wealthy people; she's identifying those who are prideful—those who put money, themselves, or other idols above the Lord. By contrast, those who are humble—hungry for God's grace and goodness—He satisfies.

It's easy for me to believe God will supply in times of need. It's when I'm flourishing that I don't always remember to acknowledge that God is the one who provides all things. But even when we are thriving we can learn to walk with a God-honoring attitude. Whether rich or poor, it's when our hearts are humble that we see God most clearly and experience His grace.

Father, show me where my pride is in the way of Your grace. I want to walk in the peace and joy of a humble heart today. In Jesus' name, amen.

December 27

Adjust Your Gaze

When you enter the land the L{ord} your God is giving you, do not learn to imitate the detestable ways of the nations there (Deuteronomy 18:9).

Scripture: Deuteronomy 18:9-14
Song: "Turn Your Eyes upon Jesus"

Sitting in a room that had just gone from light to dark, my husband turned on a light, and our eyes took a moment to adjust. It was amazing how quickly our eyes had adjusted to the dark. In the darkness, the iris opens the pupil as wide as possible. This allows us to see more in the dark.

It's like what can happen to our perspective when it comes to the things of this world. If the people of Israel were not careful to keep their eyes on the instructions God had given them, they would quickly become accustomed to and accepting of the culture around them. The land was full of idol worship and wicked practices. Israel needed to stay focused, or they'd quickly entertain evil. It's the same for us as Christians. If we take our eyes off Jesus and His narrow way, our spiritual eyes can quickly grow accustomed to an array of sinful thinking and behavior that we previously would not have accepted.

The ways of the world do not please the Lord. Let's not compromise our morals or values by "playing" with the world. By keeping our gaze fixed on Christ, we'll retain our integrity as we seek to honor our Savior in all that we do.

Father, today as I refocus on You, please wash me clean of any worldly influences. In Jesus' name, amen.

December 28

Don't Doubt

When they saw [Jesus], they worshiped him; but some doubted (Matthew 28:17).

Scripture: Matthew 28:16-20
Song: "No Doubt About It"

When we had our puppy spayed, she had a couple of days when she just wasn't feeling well and wasn't her hyper self. Our three children were worried and asked multiple times, "Will she be like this forever?" Each time, their dad and I assured them that she would be fine in a few days, but they were skeptical because what we were promising was so different from what they were seeing in the moment.

The disciples saw Jesus perform great miracles, so shouldn't it have been easy for them to believe He was the Messiah and that one day He would die and rise again, just as He said He would? Of course, they didn't have the New Testament Scriptures to tell them what would happen next. They were just going by what they saw happening in the moment, and it didn't line up with how they thought things should be. So for some of Jesus' followers, doubt crept in.

It's easy for us to say we believe the Bible is the Word of God. But do we believe it's true in *our* lives? What about when we receive a tough diagnosis? Or another large bill arrives? Or we see a loved one go astray? Do we allow doubt to creep in and tell us things just aren't supposed to be this way? God's Word promises that He is working all things together for our good (Romans 8:28). Will we believe Him?

Father, I will trust You. In Jesus' name, amen.

December 29

Known by God

Listen to me, you islands; hear this, you distant nations: Before I was born the Lord called me; from my mother's womb he has spoken my name (Isaiah 49:1).

Scripture: Isaiah 49:1-6
Song: "All My Ways Are Known to You"

"Don't call me 'Baby.' My name is Gideon!" my 7-year-old shouted. One thing he despises is for anyone to call him anything other than his name. He has one exception: me. I can call him "Gid-Gid" or "Buddy" or any other endearing name. Perhaps it's because he knows that I truly know him (as well as a mom can know a child). He knows that he doesn't have to explain that he is Gideon to me.

In today's verse we read Isaiah's prophecy regarding the Messiah's calling and identity and that both were established long before His birth. Actually, this verse may remind us of other passages about God's knowing a person's identity before they were born: Jeremiah 1:5, Psalm 139:16, and Galatians 1:15 all speak in these terms. It's comforting to know that those who belong to God are known and called and seen by Him.

God has known us from eternity past. He sees each one of us, and He calls us by name. We are His children and joint heirs with Christ in His kingdom to come. In Christ we are redeemed and set apart. Let's celebrate today knowing that we are known by Him and called to serve in His kingdom forever!

Father, thank You that You call me Your child. Thank You that my identity is found in You. I'll rest in this tremendous truth today. In Jesus' name, amen.

December 30

Light of the World

"Arise, shine, for your light has come, and the glory of the Lord rises upon you" (Isaiah 60:1).

Scripture: Isaiah 60:1-6
Song: "Shine, Jesus, Shine"

"Rise and shine and give God the glory, glory" were some of my favorite song lyrics as a child. I didn't understand the impact of the words at the time, but I enjoyed singing such a catchy tune. However, it's probably one of the reasons Psalm 34:5—"Those who look to him are radiant"—is one of my go-to Bible verses today. I love anything that reminds me that, as a Christian, I am to let my light shine.

Isaiah 59 paints a dark picture of coming wrath and much suffering. But to those who believe in the Lord, Isaiah 60:2 gives great hope. "See, darkness covers the earth and thick darkness is over the peoples, but the Lord rises upon you and his glory appears over you."

Because of Christ, the light of salvation has come into this dark world, and one day the darkness of sin and death will come to an end! As believers, we are to radiate God's love in this sullen world, proclaiming the light of the gospel wherever we go. We know that the darkness of this world won't last forever. So let's keep our eyes on the one who helps us spread His hope.

Father, thank You for Your light that is a beacon and lamp for me in this evil world. Help me to share the light of Your truth so that others might draw near to You. In Jesus' name, amen.

December 31

Rerouting Us Again

Having been warned in a dream not to go back to Herod, they returned to their country by another route (Matthew 2:12).

Scripture: Matthew 2:1-12
Song: "Leaning on the Everlasting Arms"

"She's rerouting us again, Mom?" my daughter questioned with a slight grin. She knows all too well that her mama is directionally challenged. Google Maps will tell me to go right, and I automatically turn left. It will tell me to turn left, and I take a right. It happens way too often for my liking. The good news? Whether I miss one turn or ten, the result is always the same: we reach our destination. (It may just take longer than we anticipated.)

I imagine the magi may have felt a little discouraged when they had to return to their country by another route. I'm sure they had chosen the quickest or perhaps easiest way when following the star. Their return may have been tedious and exhausting. The route may have been unsafe. However, they did it for the result: avoiding King Herod and obeying God.

Maybe this year's journey took you on a route you didn't expect, and you're leery of what's ahead. Maybe you're weary of the twists and turns, and maybe you're skeptical of what's to come. Rest in Jesus, knowing that He orders our steps (Psalm 37:23). You will arrive at the destination He has for you.

Father, thank You for directing my path, even when the route seems scary. Help me to trust in You every step of the way. In Jesus' name, amen.

January 1

Boundary Lines

The LORD is our judge, the LORD is our lawgiver, the LORD is our king; it is he who will save us (Isaiah 33:22).

Scripture: Isaiah 33:15-22
Song: "All Hail the Power of Jesus' Name"

When I was a child, I loved jumping off of my brother's bunk bed. I was upset when my mother put a stop to it, so behind her back I sought my father's permission. When my parents discovered my trickery, my father had a long conversation with me about honesty and about why rules exist. In this case, my mother was worried that my recklessness might lead to a broken bone.

It can be tempting to think of boundaries as arbitrary joy-killers. But good boundaries in our households, in games, in relationships, and in the workplace are essential. Such rules exist to benefit us, not to harm us.

God has set moral boundaries so we can flourish. We might think that if we were God, we would draw the boundary lines differently in some cases, but we cannot see what He sees. Our Heavenly Father can see the whole picture—the purpose of all He has created, the consequences of our actions, and the best road for our thriving and wholeness. It pleases Him when we trust that the lines exist because He delights in us.

Father, thank You that You set boundaries for my protection so I can thrive. In Jesus' name, amen.

January 1–7. **Julie Smyth** lives in Colorado Springs, Colorado, and serves in the evangelism and student ministries at her church. She enjoys hiking and long walks with her dog, Peaches.

January 2

Faith That Remembers

We have sinned, even as our ancestors did; . . . Yet [God] saved them for his name's sake, to make his mighty power known (Psalm 106:6, 8).

Scripture: Psalm 106:1-12
Song: "O God, Our Help in Ages Past"

One Saturday I received a call from the veterinarian's office about picking up some medication for my dog. After the receptionist explained the options, I asked, "What hours are you open today?" With an awkward chuckle, she repeated what she had said less than 15 seconds before. I had already forgotten!

Forgetting comes easily; remembering is harder. And our minds can play tricks on us. We may remember trivial things while letting go of important ones. We may hold onto painful memories and forget pleasant ones. Or perhaps we paint the past in rosy hues while seeing the present only in shades of gray. We might become so overwhelmed by current challenges that we forget what God has already done.

Today's passage recounts Israel's past and how, despite their faults and challenges, God protected them, saved them, and forgave them. His love for His people was not dependent on their perfection but on His own character and faithfulness. His love for us is steadfast as well. Just like our spiritual predecessors, we often stumble into sin or face overwhelming challenges. Yet we can fully trust that the same God who was faithful in the past will remain faithful now and always.

Father, recounting Your faithfulness bolsters my faith. I praise You for all Your goodness to me. In Jesus' name, amen.

January 3

A Better Reward

[Moses] regarded disgrace for the sake of Christ as of greater value than the treasures of Egypt, because he was looking ahead to his reward (Hebrews 11:26).

Scripture: Hebrews 11:20-29
Song: "Standing on the Promises"

The 1972 Stanford Marshmallow Experiments tested preschool children's ability to delay gratification. In one of the tests, researchers had 50 children divided into five groups. Some of them were told that if they could wait 15 minutes, they would receive their preferred treat—a choice between a marshmallow and a pretzel. If they did not wait the entire time, they would receive the less-desirable treat. Each group had a different protocol, making the challenge of waiting more or less difficult. Some children waited, while others just couldn't. Interestingly, long-term follow-up studies suggested that the children who were able to wait longer tended to have better outcomes later in life, both academically and behaviorally.

Delaying gratification can be hard, whether it entails waiting to eat a tasty marshmallow, begin married life, achieve career goals, or make purchases. Responsible living often requires us to put off what we want now so that we can attain something better in the long run. When we remember future rewards as we pursue our present ambitions, waiting becomes a little easier.

This world offers many temporary pleasures, but none compare to the surpassing beauty and goodness of our Savior. We know that if we hold fast to our calling and faith, one day we will see Jesus face to face. What could be better?

Father, I'm looking forward to the reward You promise. You are my greatest joy. In Jesus' name, amen.

January 4

A Lasting Legacy

These [men and women] were all commended for their faith, yet none of them received what had been promised (Hebrews 11:39).

Scripture: Hebrews 11:32-40
Song: "Great Is Thy Faithfulness"

Two framed pictures hang in my grandparents' kitchen: one of an elderly man seated at a table praying and the other of an elderly woman, mirroring the man's posture. Those inexpensive prints represent a rich reality: two people—my grandparents—who have faithfully prayed for their children, grandchildren, and great-grandchildren. Their daily prayers are the foundation of a legacy of faith passed down to three generations.

If each of us painted a portrait to represent our life, what would it look like? We usually speak of a person's legacy at the end of their life. In reality, our legacies begin taking shape much sooner than that. From a young age, we make daily choices that shape our character, laying the groundwork for our final legacy. Even those who have no children touch the lives of those around them for better or for worse.

Perhaps some of the best questions we can ask ourselves at any age are: *What kind of legacy do I want to leave behind?* and *What kind of legacy pleases God?* Our faith blossoms when we begin intentionally building our lives around loving Jesus and introducing people to Him. Faith, joy, and grace leave a lasting imprint on those who follow us as we follow Christ.

Father, as I learn to walk in daily obedience to You, I'll seek to leave a legacy for future generations of those who love You. In Jesus' name, amen.

January 5

Prone to Wander

[God] took note of [His people's] distress when he heard their cry; for their sake he remembered his covenant and out of his great love he relented (Psalm 106:44-45).

Scripture: Psalm 106:13, 26-27, 42-48
Song: "Blessed Assurance"

Andrew van der Bijl mastered the art of playing hooky from church. As a boy, he'd feign graciousness, giving up his seat. Then he'd stand in the back of the overcrowded sanctuary. From there he'd sneak out and could masterfully trick everyone into believing he had attended the service. Van der Bijl disregarded faith for many years and lived wildly as a soldier in the Dutch army in Indonesia. After being crippled by a bullet, he cried out to God from a repentant heart. In time, van der Bijl became known as "God's Smuggler"—a name he earned sneaking Bibles into Communist countries during the Cold War.

Repentance is a key part of vibrant Christian faith. Like the father of a prodigal, God is ready to respond to the cries of the contrite. We must not be afraid to call on our Heavenly Father after stumbling—or even diving head-first—into sin. He hears our distress, extends mercy, and encompasses us with His great love.

Some sins can seem unforgiveable, as though God's grace has been stretched too far. But when our pride and fear tell us Jesus' blood cannot cover our sins, we are wrong. No matter how deep someone has descended into darkness, God is always ready to deliver the one who calls on Him.

Father, thank You for Your grace. I want to repent from sin quickly and walk in obedience. In Jesus' name, amen.

January 6

The Sweetest Gift

The law was brought in so that the trespass might increase. But where sin increased, grace increased all the more (Romans 5:20).

Scripture: Romans 5:12-21
Song: "Amazing Grace"

I did not enjoy spicy food when I was young. I couldn't understand why any right-minded person would add extra jalapeños or hot salsa to their food. Yet my mother did it routinely. I avoided spicy foods until my teen years. That's when my mother told me a secret: spicy foods make dessert taste even sweeter.

Extra spicy chili may be a poor analogy for sin, but it illustrates a key point. Many people today feel that honest conversations about sin make God or Christianity sound unloving. It's true that sin is an uncomfortable topic for us, since we are *all* guilty before God! But it's also true that the seriousness of our moral failings makes the good news of His grace and mercy all the sweeter.

God welcomes a broken and contrite heart (Psalm 51:17), and it is His joy to exercise grace toward the humble (James 4:6). Sometimes humility can be hard to come by. However, when we look up at a mountain's grandeur, we don't need to manufacture awe or strive for humility. Our humility is a sincere response to the majesty of what's in view. In a similar way, when we keep our eyes fixed on the sweetness of God's grace and kindness, we become able to respond to Him from a truly humble heart.

Father, as I focus on the greatness of Your grace right now, please soften my heart to receive it. In Jesus' name, amen.

January 7

Eyes Wide Open

Faith is confidence in what we hope for and assurance about what we do not see (Hebrews 11:1).

Scripture: Hebrews 11:1-4, 7-8, 17-18, 20-23, 32, 39-40
Song: "By Faith"

When I was a teenager, "trust falls" were a popular youth-group activity. One teen was expected to fall backward, trusting another teen standing behind her to break the fall. I hated trust falls. In fact, the only person I would do a trust fall with was my father. Blindly trusting another teenager scared me. But I had faith in my father. I had ample evidence of his good character. He would keep his promise to catch me.

Many people today confuse the word *faith* with the idea of blindly believing without a good reason. But this is not how the Scriptures define faith. Faith is trust in what is yet unseen, based on the evidence of who God is and what He has already done.

The prophets believed God would send a Savior *because* they had seen God keep His promises. The disciples believed in the resurrection and the gospel message *because* they saw Jesus die and then rise again, as He said He would. The evidence they saw gave them confidence in what they did not yet see. Today and in the future, we too can have confident faith *because* of the disciples' carefully recorded eyewitness testimony. Our faith is not blind; our faith is trust in a proven Savior.

Father, thank You for giving me all that I need for confident faith in all You have done and will do. In Jesus' name, amen.

January 8

Navigating Life's Obstacles

Thy word is a lamp unto my feet (Psalm 119:105, *KJV*).

Scripture: Psalm 119:97-112
Song: "Thy Word"

On the popular, long-running reality television program *Survivor*, contestants face off in various challenges to win rewards, such as food, blankets, and immunity from getting voted off the show. In one recurring challenge, contestants must work as a team to complete tasks within an obstacle course.

This challenge is difficult because the team members completing the tasks are blindfolded. The only way they know what to do is by listening to the voice of the "caller"—the one person who can see what is going on. The caller's ability to give clear directions and the other contestants' ability to listen carefully, precisely following the caller's instructions, mean the difference between victory and defeat.

None of us knows what the future holds. Often it feels as though life is an obstacle course that we're trying to navigate blindfolded! Thankfully, God's Word provides us with a manual for life, helping us avoid pitfalls and teaching us how to please Him in all we do. Our responsibility is to listen carefully and trust His instructions, obeying them even when we can't see the outcome. This is what it means to live a life of faith.

Father, remind me today that living a life of faith means following You even when I cannot see the way forward. In Jesus' name, amen.

January 8–14. **Kelly VanKirk Suzano** lives in New York State with her husband and daughter. She teaches chorus and general music classes and helps lead worship at her local church.

January 9

The Outcome Is His

[Jesus said,] "My yoke is easy and my burden is light" (Matthew 11:30).

Scripture: Matthew 11:25-30
Song: "I Cast All My Cares upon You"

I owned a Christian dance studio for several years, and while I loved my job, it was nerve-racking to have an entire year of teaching evaluated based on a single performance by my students. Without fail each year—a few weeks before our big, end-of-the-year recital—I would start having anxious dreams. Once I even dreamed that my students spilled soda pop all over the studio floor and then used their recital costumes to clean up the mess!

The problem was that no matter how well I prepared, the outcome was never totally in my hands. One unfocused dancer could derail a performance, and it was this feeling of not being in control that produced all my stress-induced nightmares.

We can be thankful that God has a better way for us to go about our lives and our work in His kingdom. When we take His yoke, *He* carries the burden, so there is no pressure on us to perform. We can plant gospel seeds in the hearts of our unsaved friends and family, pray for our children night and day, and share the truths of God's Word with everyone we meet. But at the end of the day, it's God's Spirit who causes our work to succeed. What a relief to know that, by faith, we can place our work in His hands and trust Him with the outcome.

Father, thank You that I can rest, knowing that my work in Your kingdom is in Your hands. In Jesus' name, amen.

January 10

Prison with a Purpose

When I am afraid, I put my trust in you (Psalm 56:3).

Scripture: Psalm 56
Song: "Faith of Our Fathers"

In 1660, Puritan minister John Bunyan (1628–1688) was arrested for conducting religious meetings in Bedford, England. (A newly restored monarchy deemed such gatherings illegal.) He was held in prison for refusing to give up preaching and spent the majority of the next 12 years suffering under the conditions of his confinement, separated from his wife and children. Despite these hardships, Bunyan chose to follow in the footsteps of the apostles. He knew from their example that he "ought to obey God rather than men" (Acts 5:29, *KJV*).

The apostle Paul was arrested for preaching the gospel too. It was likely during one of his detainments in Rome that he wrote the books of Ephesians, Philippians, Colossians, and Philemon. Bunyan, like Paul, used his prison time to write, penning many sermons and various titles, including his most famous book, *The Pilgrim's Progress*. Considered one of the greatest works of theological fiction in the English language, this allegory has been a source of encouragement to Christians for more than three centuries.

We may never find ourselves imprisoned for our faith, but at some point, we may experience what seems like an imprisonment of the soul—a time when we feel shackled by circumstances, sorrow, or anxiety. God can use these times to refine our faith, further conforming us to Christ's image. Even our prisons can be redeemed for His purposes.

Father, I trust that that You're with me in my trials and that You will bring about Your good purposes through them. In Jesus' name, amen.

Spiritual Sight

We are looking for the city that is to come (Hebrews 13:14).

Scripture: Hebrews 13:5-16
Song: "O Love That Wilt Not Let Me Go"

George Matheson (1842–1906) was a popular 19th-century Scottish preacher. His sermons were powerful and moving, but many who heard him speak had no idea of the private burden he bore. As a young man, George began losing his eyesight, and soon all he could see were shadows. To make matters worse, when the woman to whom he was engaged found out about his condition, she called off their wedding. On the evening of his sister's wedding, George was feeling particularly burdened. Perhaps the wedding brought up memories of his lost relationship. Whatever it was, his pain inspired him to pen the much-beloved hymn "O Love That Wilt Not Let Me Go."

One of the main themes of the book of Hebrews is that the physical world is simply a shadow of the real world, Heaven. George knew that this world was not his home, and through the eyes of faith, he saw a heavenly city where all tears would one day be wiped away. He trusted that God's love and care for him were strong enough to overcome any burden in this life.

May the words he penned encourage our hearts to look to Heaven too: "O Joy that seekest me through pain, / I cannot close my heart to Thee. / I trace the rainbow through the rain, / And feel the promise is not vain, / That morn shall tearless be."

Father, by faith I will fix my gaze on the things of Heaven. In Jesus' name, amen.

January 12

Mother to Thousands

[Jesus said,] I will not leave you as orphans; I will come to you (John 14:18).

Scripture: John 14:18-27
Song: "I Surrender All"

In her early twenties, Lillian Trasher (1887–1961) was 10 days away from marrying the love of her life. There was just one problem: she had a growing belief that God was calling her to be a missionary, and her future husband did not share her conviction. In the most difficult decision of her young life, she broke off her engagement and committed herself to becoming a missionary.

On October 8, 1910, Trasher set sail for Alexandria, Egypt, trusting that God would show her what to do when she got there. Within months of arriving, the young missionary was called upon to pray at the deathbed of a mother with a young infant. Trasher felt compelled to take the child in. She was soon renting her own house and taking in more orphans, providing food, shelter, and the love of Christ to Cairo's most vulnerable. Although it may have seemed to Lillian Trasher that she had given up her dream of having a family, she became a mother to thousands!

God calls each of us to "die" to our own goals and ambitions so that His purposes can be accomplished through us. When we loosen our grip on our own plans, we open ourselves to discovering the life God has planned for us—a life lived for God's highest glory and the greatest good in this world.

Father, thank You for providing the grace and strength I need to surrender all to You. In Jesus' name, amen.

His Spirit Speaks

We have the mind of Christ (1 Corinthians 2:16).

Scripture: 1 Corinthians 2:6-16
Song: "All the Way My Savior Leads Me"

Many years ago, I had the privilege of having a meal with a survivor of a North Korean prison camp. I listened in awe as this woman described her experiences. She was not a Christian when she was first arrested, but God revealed himself to her and she received Christ as Savior. In her newfound faith, she had neither a Bible nor any Christian mentors, but the Spirit of God began revealing truth to her, showing her how He wanted her to live. It wasn't until after her escape that she realized the Holy Spirit had revealed many truths of Scripture to her, even though she had no physical copy of God's Word.

What a reproof her story brought to my heart! Although I had numerous Bibles, how often did I truly take time out of my day to meditate on God's Word and allow its truth to penetrate my heart? How often did I quiet myself long enough to know the conviction of God's Spirit?

As Christians, we are heirs to incredible promises; one of the most humbling is that we have been given the mind of Christ. Let's not take this for granted but daily immerse ourselves in God's holy Word instead. When we do, God's truth will begin to change us from within.

Father, thank You for the gift of Your Word and the power of Your Holy Spirit in my life! I will be careful not to take these for granted. In Jesus' name, amen.

January 14

Stepping Out in Faith

In all your ways submit to him, and he will make your paths straight (Proverbs 3:6).

Scripture: Proverbs 3:1-12
Song: "Trust and Obey"

When I was in college, I believed that God was directing me to go to China and teach English for the summer. But I wanted to be sure I was following His lead. I prayed. I sought counsel. I pleaded for God to give me a sign so I would *know*. Then one day, while at the laundromat, I noticed a small booklet on a table. It was about the need for the gospel in China. What clearer sign did I need? Still, I hesitated. How can one really *know* they are in the will of God?

Something my dad said to me not only made me decide to go to China but also freed me from years of hesitating to act because of fear. He said to me, "Kelly, you truly want God's will, and He knows that. Even if you find out later that going to China wasn't His perfect will for you, don't you trust that He's big enough to handle it?" I was dumbstruck. God wasn't asking me to make perfect decisions. He was asking me to trust my imperfect decisions to a perfect God.

As you enter the unknown of 2024, don't let fear hold you back from what you believe God is directing you to do. If you've prayed diligently and your motivation is to honor Him, step out fearlessly, trusting that God will lead you into all He has in store.

Father, I entrust my imperfect decisions to Your perfect plan. In Jesus' name, amen.

January 15

Comfort Conduit

Praise be to the God and Father of our Lord Jesus Christ ... who comforts us in all our troubles, so that we can comfort those in any trouble with the comfort we ourselves receive from God (2 Corinthians 1:3-4).

Scripture: 2 Corinthians 1:3-11
Song: "What a Friend We Have in Jesus"

At the cemetery, friends hugged me as I sobbed ugly sobs. "I know how you feel," many whispered into my ear as they drew near. Some did not, but some did, especially those whose parents were in Heaven too.

Paul was no stranger to suffering. He elaborated in 2 Corinthians 11:23-27: imprisonment, beatings, shipwreck, floggings, and hunger were a few of the things he endured. Paul and his companions also experienced grave danger in Asia, a crisis so serious they feared death (2 Corinthians 1:8-9). Rather than despair, though, Paul relied on God and considered the circumstance an opportunity to minister to others.

The troubles we face may not compare to Paul's, but God is present during our trials just the same. Perhaps our struggles involve job loss, loneliness, health issues, hurting relationships, or the challenges of aging. Whatever our greatest need might be, God is our comforter. Like Paul, our circumstances can empower us to encourage and comfort others. Let's have a faith that pleases God and share that compassion with those who need it.

Father, thank You for comforting me with such compassion. Help me be a conduit of Your love to the hurting. In Jesus' name, amen.

January 15–21. **Barbara Gordon** is a retired school teacher. Her favorite pastime is playing with grandkids.

January 16

Taste and See

Taste and see that the Lord is good; blessed is the one who takes refuge in him (Psalm 34:8).

Scripture: Psalm 34:1-10
Song: "How Great Is Our God"

My family's favorite dessert is turtle cake. Caramel, chocolate, nuts—sweet delectability! The treat is rich, moist, and mouth-watering. My children use many adjectives to describe it, but you have to taste it for yourself to understand.

Today's passage outlines several benefits of knowing God. David's psalm reminds us that God hears our prayers, delivers us from our fears, rescues us from shame, and saves us from our troubles. After detailing the rewards of following God, the psalmist encourages us not to rely on *his* experiences but to experience God's goodness for ourselves. He likens our soul's need for God to the body's need for food. And as we experience God's protection, wisdom, peace, and forgiveness firsthand, we realize He is good, indeed!

To taste God's goodness means getting to know Him personally. The first step is coming to Him through the atoning work of Jesus, His Son. Then as we read and study the Bible, pray, and listen to godly wisdom, we feed our relationship with Him. As He fills us with His goodness, we learn that we can take refuge in Him. As we experience Him for ourselves and learn to trust Him fully, our faith grows, and we come to know the sweetness of His love.

Father, I want to draw close to You and seek You in every circumstance. Thank You that I can trust Your faithfulness. You *are* good. In Jesus' name, amen.

January 17

The Heart Healer

The LORD is close to the brokenhearted (Psalm 34:18).

Scripture: Psalm 34:11-22
Song: "Abide with Me"

My first pet was a black-and-white mutt that unexpectedly showed up one summer afternoon when I was about five years old. Despite her homely appearance, I fell in love with her at the first wag of her fluffy tail. I promptly named her Poochie, and we spent hours roaming the backyard. Hot evenings we sat on the porch together as I counted fireflies and ran my fingers through her fur. When Poochie didn't survive being run over by a car, I was grief-stricken. My mom tenderly held me on her lap and rocked me while I cried.

David was well acquainted with grief and in need of a comforter too. He mourned over his sin with Bathsheba, the death of an infant son, and the betrayal of friends and family. David's psalms outline his reactions to his many losses. In them he acknowledged his heartache, cried out to God, and chose to put his faith in the one who was always there for him. Experience taught him the truth of today's passage: God is near to those whose hearts are broken.

Maybe you are brokenhearted over the loss of a loved one, a relationship, or a dream. The very same God who was close to David in his heartache draws near to us in our sorrow as well. In the midst of our despair, we can follow David's example: feel the pain, appeal to the Lord, and know that He is near.

Father, when my heart is breaking, I will look to You for comfort. In Jesus' name, amen.

January 18

Be an Encourager

Encourage one another and build each other up, just as in fact you are doing (1 Thessalonians 5:11).

Scripture: 1 Thessalonians 5:1-15
Song: "This Little Light of Mine"

I took up running on my 50th birthday. Well, maybe not *running*. Some people walk faster than I run. My goal was to one day complete a 5K race. Early on, I jogged only when I felt like it and at a speed that felt comfortable. As you might imagine, this approach didn't yield great results. Then I made a discovery: if someone ran with me, I could increase my distance and better my time. Eventually I did compete in a few 5K events, but I needed the encouragement of others to motivate me to complete that goal.

The apostle Paul used the backdrop of "the day of the Lord" to instruct believers to build up and encourage each other. Whether it's concerning the prospect of Christ's return or the uncertainty of daily life, we sometimes need reassurance. Paul indicates God's provisions for our work of encouragement: faith, love, and the hope of salvation (1 Thessalonians 5:8).

Who can we encourage today? A heartfelt note, text, or phone call might uplift another person's spirit. Praying for or with someone can provide peace and comfort and perhaps bring about a change of circumstances. Simply spending time with someone who is lonely can bring a sense of being seen and cared for. Encouraging others builds faith in both the giver and recipient.

Father, I'm grateful that You are a God of encouragement. I want to build others up as well. Show me who needs uplifting today. In Jesus' name, amen.

January 1

Choose to Rejoice *Always*

Rejoice always, pray continually, give thanks in all circumstances; for this is God's will for you in Christ Jesus (1 Thessalonians 5:16-18).

Scripture: 1 Thessalonians 5:16-28
Song: "To God Be the Glory"

Rejoice *always?* Surely the apostle Paul didn't mean *always.* When I've lost a loved one, endured medical emergencies, or mourned relationships gone bad, rejoicing has not been the theme of my prayers. I pray often, but praying *continually* seems like a stretch. Giving thanks is easy . . . unless my circumstances are crummy. But Paul says we should give thanks in *all* circumstances.

Paul teaches these three imperatives in 1 Thessalonians 5:16-18 as God's will for us. And as the one who penned these directives, Paul was no stranger to adversity. He experienced floggings, stoning, hunger, thirst, shipwreck, and many other hardships. Yet he encouraged those to whom he was writing to persist in being joyful, prayerful, and thankful even in the midst of life's very real struggles.

Our own struggles may include, among other things, a job change, relocation, relationship loss, health issues, or loss of a loved one. Such unexpected and unwanted events often create tension and grief. Yet through the ups and downs of life, the Lord remains with us, and He does not change. As we embrace Paul's principles of rejoicing, praying, and giving thanks, we will navigate the changes and challenges of life with the fullness of God's grace and strength.

Father, thank You that You fill me with Your grace and strength as my heart is continually turned toward You. In Jesus' name, amen.

January 20

Our Eyes Are on You

[King Jehoshaphat prayed,] "We do not know what to do, but our eyes are on you" (2 Chronicles 20:12).

Scripture: 2 Chronicles 20:5-12
Song: "My Hope Is in You"

Several summers ago our family vacationed at the Grand Canyon. Our adventurous agenda included hiking the nine miles to the bottom of the canyon, spending the night in a tent, then climbing out the next day. All went as planned until we encountered a flash flood on our way back up. Car-sized rocks tumbled around us as we sat on a ledge, paralyzed with fear. When the ground stabilized a bit, a park ranger came through and gathered all the hikers to a central location to walk the rest of the way out together. We kept our eyes on this ranger. He knew what we needed to do to get to safety.

King Jehoshaphat turned his eyes to God when he learned that a vast army was about to attack. The king's response to the frightening report was to pray. With the people of Judah gathered around, Jehoshaphat ended his prayer to the one who could save them with these profound words: "We do not know what to do, but our eyes are on you" (2 Chronicles 20:12).

When choked with fear and indecision, we can pray the words of Jehoshaphat with confidence. Turning our eyes to the Lord and admitting our helplessness invites His intervention in our distress. As we look to Him, He will meet us and see us through.

Father, when I don't know my next step, I will look to You and call on You. In Jesus' name, amen.

January 21

The Battle Is Not Yours

[Jahaziel said to King Jehoshaphat,] "This is what the Lord says to you: 'Do not be afraid or discouraged because of this vast army. For the battle is not yours, but God's'" (2 Chronicles 20:15).

Scripture: 2 Chronicles 20:13-20
Song: "Because He Lives"

Every year I look forward to the first hummingbird of the season. The feeder hanging outside my kitchen window has six ports with perches, which ought to be plenty for the three or four birds I have each year. Apparently, though, hummingbirds are among the most territorial of birds. Within two or three days of their arrival, the fighting begins. The most aggressive one dives and chases any other bird that tries to take a sip of the sweet solution. The feeder is never empty, but "Boss Hog," as we call him, has an agenda and is determined to win the battle at all costs.

Jehoshaphat's "Boss Hog" enemies were on their way, and the odds did not look good for Judah's king. He prayed, though, and God answered. Jehoshaphat did not have a plan, but the Lord did. First, God told the king not to be afraid. The next steps were to march, stand firm, and watch. God's people did just that, and when they finished their march, they found that the enemy armies had already destroyed each other.

Jehoshaphat's experience reminds me to bring my fears and trials to the Lord. He is faithful and able to see me through absolutely any physical or spiritual battle.

Father, I will choose to trust You and not be afraid. I know You are always with me. In Jesus' name, amen.

January 22

Faith from the Heart

[God said,] **I will take the stony heart out of their flesh, and will give them an heart of flesh** (Ezekiel 11:19, *KJV*).

Scripture: Ezekiel 11:17-21
Song: "O for a Heart to Praise My God"

Who would take a beating for a favorite shirt? Mike Christian did. But his was no ordinary shirt. With a bamboo needle, Christian—an American prisoner of war in Vietnam—had sewn a rough version of the Stars and Stripes on it. He then hung his makeshift flag in a corner of his cell and, with his patriotic cellmates, would recite the Pledge of Allegiance. When the Vietcong discovered this, they took the flag-shirt away and beat Christian mercilessly. His response? He began sewing a flag on *another* shirt. For Christian, his difficult circumstances couldn't change the love in his heart for his country.

Ezekiel ministered to the Israelite exiles in Babylon. Although God allowed Israel to go into captivity because of sin, He sent Ezekiel with a message of hope. One day, the Lord would gather His people to their land again and give them a new heart—one that would follow God faithfully.

We too may feel knocked down and beaten up by circumstances in life. But God has given us a new heart that can sustain us through any trial. When our hearts are filled with love for God, the faithfulness it produces honors Him.

Father, thank You for a new heart by which I can seek to please You. In Jesus' name, amen.

January 22–28. **David Madsen** lives in Wisconsin with his family. He teaches English at a Christian college.

January 23

Faith Through Seeing God Work

[The man born blind] answered and said, Whether he be a sinner or no, I know not: one thing I know, that, whereas I was blind, now I see (John 9:25, *KJV*).

Scripture: John 9:17-25
Song: "God Will Take Care of You"

God's timing is perfect . . . even when we don't see Him working until the last minute. Author Solomon Benjamin Shaw (1854–1941) recounted the story of a poor frontier pastor and his wife who had nothing for their children at Christmastime. Listening to their little daughter's prayer for a doll for herself and skates for her brothers broke their hearts, as they knew she would be disappointed. The couple began doubting God's care for them until a knock at the door on Christmas Eve brought an unexpected box of goodies from a church back East—including a doll and skates! Seeing God work in their situation renewed their faith.

After Jesus gave sight to a blind man, this man was brought before the Pharisees for questioning. Despite the Pharisees' obvious hostility toward Jesus and their disbelief in His deity, the man pointed out the undeniable: Jesus had given him his sight! The Savior's work in His life gave Him faith that Jesus was who He said.

Discouragement and doubt can easily creep into our lives amid life's disappointments. Yet when we consider the times when we have seen God's work in our lives through answered prayer, unexpected blessings, or divine provision, we can more easily entrust our lives to His loving care.

Father, thank You for Your work in my life that encourages my faith. In Jesus' name, amen.

January 24

Trusting God's Directions

Ye shall inherit their land, and I will give it unto you to possess it, a land that floweth with milk and honey: I am the LORD your God, which have separated you from other people (Leviticus 20:24, *KJV*).

Scripture: Leviticus 20:22-26
Song: "Trusting Jesus"

Running out of gas can be a problem—especially at 4,000 feet in the air! My former pastor told of such a harrowing experience as navigator in a large World War II bomber. Returning from a mission, the plane was desperately trying to reach an aircraft carrier before running out of fuel and crashing into the ocean. But thick clouds meant zero visibility, and the commander expressed doubt the navigation equipment was taking them in the right direction. Yet just before expending the last of the fuel, the plane broke through the clouds in sight of the carrier and landed safely. The navigator's directions were right after all!

When God brought the Israelites out of Egypt, He promised them a land flowing with milk and honey. The Lord himself would cast out the ungodly inhabitants so that Israel could walk in obedience to Him without hindrance. Sadly, the Israelites doubted God's plan, fearing the land's inhabitants, and Israel rebelled, consequently spending the next 40 years wandering in the wilderness.

God has given us the Bible as our compass for life. However, sometimes our own notions and ideas may tempt us to doubt His plan. But God's directions can always be trusted to lead us the right way, and He is pleased when we follow Him in faith.

Father, help me to trust the directions You have given me in Your Word. In Jesus' name, amen.

January 25

A Heart of Repentance

Restore unto me the joy of thy salvation; and uphold me with thy free spirit (Psalm 51:12, KJV).

Scripture: Psalm 51:1-15
Song: "Create in Me a Clean Heart"

Old dogs really can learn new tricks . . . and old politicians can even learn new values! Former Alabama Governor George Wallace (1919–1998) went down in infamy for his hostile defense of racial segregation in the 1960s. However, Wallace, who served a total of four terms as governor, surrendered his life to Christ in the late 1970s, resulting in a complete change of heart on race issues. He admitted he was wrong to support segregation, and he appointed record numbers of Black professionals to important state offices. True repentance resulted in a genuine change.

After Nathan the prophet confronted David about his adultery with Bathsheba and the murder of Uriah, her husband, David repented of his sin. Psalm 51 records David's complete confession of his wrongdoing, his plea for God's forgiveness, and his desire to be renewed in fellowship with the Lord. Although David had to bear harsh consequences for his sin, his true repentance resulted in a genuine change—a contrite and broken heart before the Lord.

True repentance from sin always produces real change in our lives. God is gracious and, when we fall, He is waiting to forgive and restore us. As with David, honestly confessing our sin and calling on God for restoration will result in a changed heart that brings forth what is well-pleasing to God.

Father, help me to truly repent when I sin so that my relationship with You can be restored. In Jesus' name, amen.

January 26

The God of the Impossible

[God] said unto me, Son of man, can these bones live? And I answered, O Lord God, thou knowest (Ezekiel 37:3, KJV).

Scripture: Ezekiel 37:1-14
Song: "God Can Do Anything"

Leading elephants over snow-capped mountains may not make sense to us, but it made perfect sense to Hannibal Barca (247–182 BC). The famous commander of Carthage's army made a daring move to surprise the Romans during the Second Punic War (218–201 BC). He set out to take his army—including dozens of war elephants—from Spain to Italy by going over the dangerous Alps, a route thought impassable. This surprise move helped Carthage win decisive battles against Rome and made Hannibal one of the greatest military strategists in history.

During Ezekiel's ministry, God showed the prophet a valley full of dry human bones. With this evidence of death all around, the Lord asked Ezekiel whether the bones could live again. To Ezekiel, the question may not have made sense, and he wisely replied that only God could know the answer. By His sovereign power, God brought the bones together, placed flesh on them, and breathed life into the bodies. What seemed impossible was possible with the Lord.

As believers, we may sometimes face seemingly impossible situations. There might even be times when the instructions God provides in His Word and the Holy Spirit's guidance don't seem to make sense to us. Yet we can trust that whatever God calls us to do, He is able to accomplish it, making even the impossible possible.

Father, I praise You for Your power to do what is impossible. In Jesus' name, amen.

Living Out God's Love

Hereby perceive we the love of God, because he laid down his life for us: and we ought to lay down our lives for the brethren (1 John 3:16, *KJV*).

Scripture: 1 John 3:14-24
Song: "This Is My Commandment"

In 1878, England experienced a diphtheria epidemic, and not even the royal family escaped its ravages. All but one of Princess Alice's children contracted the disease, and although she tried to care for them, she was careful to avoid physical contact. However, when her daughter Marie was the first to die, her son Ernest became so distraught that Alice comforted him with a kiss. This may have resulted in the princess contracting the disease herself, and she succumbed to it not long after. But to Alice, *love* meant caring for her children in their time of greatest need, regardless of personal cost.

In his first letter, the apostle John encouraged believers to live out their faith by giving to the needy in their midst. He noted that just as God demonstrated His love in sending Christ to die for us, so Christians should show their love for one another by caring for each other selflessly. John clearly teaches that love is not a theory but a sacrificial action to meet practical needs.

As believers, we are called to look for opportunities to help our sisters and brothers in Christ. Like God's sacrificial love for us, we can demonstrate our love by generous action toward others, knowing that this pleases the Lord.

Father, help us to love one another as You have loved us. In Jesus' name, amen.

January 28

Exercising Our Gifts

We, being many, are one body in Christ, and every one members one of another (Romans 12:5, *KJV*).

Scripture: Romans 12:3-8
Song: "The Family of God"

Billy Graham (1918–2018) was a household name for decades. The world-famous evangelist preached in auditoriums and stadiums around the world. But most people may not know that his first sermon as an 18-year-old was less than inspiring and lasted only eight minutes. After that experience, Graham "wrestled with God" about his calling to preach but finally obeyed. His autobiography discloses that he would paddle his canoe to a little island where he practiced his preaching skills on whatever audience was at hand—alligators, birds, or even cypress stumps.

The apostle Paul told the believers in Rome that God had gifted each of them in different ways. Like the human body has many parts—all of which are needed—Paul said that each believer's gift is important and needed for the Church to function well. As such, Paul encouraged the believers to exercise their gifts, recognizing that they were given by God and could be a blessing to others.

In the same way, believers today should put their gifts into practice so that the church can be edified. Believers can be confident that whatever gifts He has given are an important part of His work in this world. Regardless of how God wants to use our gifts, we can be assured that actively exercising them for the Lord's work will produce fruit for eternity.

Father, help me to use my gifts to glorify You. In Jesus' name, amen.

January 29

Measuring God's Love

I pray that you, being rooted and established in love, may have power, together with all the Lord's holy people, to grasp how wide and long and high and deep is the love of Christ (Ephesians 3:17-18).

Scripture: Ephesians 3:14-21
Song: "The Love of God (Is Greater Far)"

Measuring devices come in all shapes and sizes, and we use them for various applications. Children experiment with rulers to draw straight lines as they learn to measure length, height, and width. Scientists use the metric system to document scientific results, while contractors rely on tape measures, speed squares, or levels to determine project specifications. Even the finest chefs in the world need a measuring spoon or two as they create divine cuisine!

Our Creator needs no measuring device to determine the amount of love He bestows upon us. When Paul addressed the church of Ephesus, he explained that the love of Christ has no depth, width, or height. With faith rooted in that love, Paul endured considerable physical and mental hardships throughout his lifetime.

We experience many hardships during our lifetimes as well. Our days are unpredictable, and we often fear financial failure, broken relationships, illness, and overwhelming emotional distress; yet our hearts remain hopeful as we seek refuge in the mighty arms of our Lord and Savior.

Father, my faith is rooted in Your unconditional love, and I'm thankful for the hope You bestow on me during trials and tribulations. In Jesus' name, amen.

January 29–February 4. **Kellie M. Everett** lives in Tennessee with her husband and children. She is a stay-at-home mom and author.

January 30

The Crashing Waves of Life

You [God] rule over the surging sea; when its waves mount up, you still them (Psalm 89:9).

Scripture: Psalm 89:1-13
Song: "O Maker of the Mighty Deep"

Virginia Beach was the setting for an incredibly interesting vacation with my husband. I can see it now—an exquisite beachfront stretched out beneath a vibrant blue sky, nestled against the vastness of the ocean's horizon. The sun was warm and gentle as it blazed brilliantly above our heads; it was pure perfection. I felt carefree jumping into the water, but I was unaware of an approaching storm, and the waves were stronger than expected. No sooner had I jumped in, than the sea tossed me right back out! (To this day, I remain "salty" about falling and losing my all-time favorite sunglasses!)

The psalmist praised the Lord for His faithfulness and promised to pass this knowledge down to future generations. He understood God to be all-powerful, all-knowledgeable, and all-present—a God whose mighty hands are powerful enough to control the surging sea. He had faith in the unconditional love of God.

Our lives can be much like my experience at the beach. We feel carefree as we frolic amidst soft, gentle waves until we fall helplessly into a thrashing surge of turmoil. In these seasons, we remember that God is in control. Our faith acquires new understanding as He lifts us out of despair and steadies our feet to continue our stroll along the shore of life.

Father, I'm thankful for Your continuing presence as You guide me. Your love is faithful and powerful, and You rescue me from dangerous storms. In Jesus' name, amen.

January 31

God's Love, a Promise Guaranteed

[God] remembers his covenant forever, the promise he made, for a thousand generations (1 Chronicles 16:15).

Scripture: 1 Chronicles 16:8-22
Song: "My Redeemer Is Faithful and True"

Worldly turmoil simmered in 1916 when President Woodrow Wilson (1856–1924) ran for and won re-election. His campaign slogan had been, "He kept us out of war." In 1914, World War I had ensued, and as conflict brewed in Europe, U.S. voters were pleased by this implicit promise to remain neutral. However, an attack on U.S. merchant ships resulted in the loss of innocent lives. Within a year of Wilson's re-election, U.S. involvement in World War I was no longer avoidable.

Our words are not always reliable; we're often fickle with our promises, sometimes with devastating consequences. Thankfully, God's promises are guaranteed! He has never broken His covenant with generations past, present, or future. In today's passage, David is thankful for God's faithfulness and, with delight in his heart, raises his hands to praise the Lord. David recounts multiple occasions of God's deliverance and directs God's people to do the same.

Time and again, God has provided refuge, comfort, and peace to His people in the midst of darkness and uncertainty. When struggles ensue, He is always present. We see His consistency and remain hopeful as He uses life's events to build character and strengthen our faith. He is committed to caring for us as we walk the path of righteousness in His presence.

Father, my faith becomes stronger each day as I remain rooted in Your love. Please use my life and words to extend Your promise of salvation to others. In Jesus' name, amen.

February 1

Life's Unpredictable Variables

[The twenty-four elders said,] "We give thanks to you, Lord God Almighty, the One who is and who was, because you have taken your great power and have begun to reign" (Revelation 11:17).

Scripture: Revelation 11:14-19
Song: "God's Love Never Changes"

I used to purchase two new Boston ferns each spring and then lament as they burnt to a crisp within a month. When I announced this chronic problem to my women's group, Mrs. Nell, one of the group's members, brought over a new Boston fern the next day. She taught me about proper sun exposure, temperature, and the importance of an efficient watering routine. She even shared her secret fish-oil mixture that virtually guaranteed success! Of the three ferns I acquired that season, the variables in their care produced very different outcomes. Only the fern nourished steadfastly with Mrs. Nell's instruction lived for many years.

Scripture tells us that the 24 elders will fall before God and praise Him with thanksgiving. Their humility reflects their reverence and the honor they feel in serving a living God whose existence is from eternity past, a God who always remains the same.

The variables in our lives are unpredictable, and everyone's experience in life is different. But as God's children we can, like that well-nurtured fern, thrive under God's wise and consistent care. No matter what comes, we can remain certain that our living God, who is eternal, remains faithful, steadfast, and loving.

Father, I cannot rely on this uncertain world for what I need; but thank You that I can find consistent refuge and care in Your love for me. In Jesus' name, amen.

Birds of a Feather

I long to see you so that I may impart to you some spiritual gift to make you strong—that is, that you and I may be mutually encouraged by each other's faith (Romans 1:11-12).

Scripture: Romans 1:8-17
Song: "Come, Let Us Join Our Friends Above"

"Birds of a feather flock together" is a proverb whose English origins can be found in a 1545 work of religious satire written by William Turner. Turner's metaphor points to the tendency of people with things in common to be drawn to one another and to spend time together.

In the world of birds, flocking behaviors provide many perks! Birds in large numbers may be able to scare away predators or confuse them by scattering. When searching for food, a flock has many eyes scanning the terrain and can more readily locate resources. Finally, birds flying together can enhance aerodynamics, aligning in a V formation during flight to conserve energy during the long migration journey.

The apostle Paul was yearning to return to his friends in Rome. He praised and encouraged them for their ability to work together in spreading the gospel message. As a group of believers, they had accomplished much in their service for the Lord.

Christian fellowship is vital. Praying together, we can fend off the enemy's attacks. As we study God's Word together, we nurture our faith. When we work together as God's people and encourage one another, we are restored and replenished along the journey to our eternal home.

Father, the spiritual community You've given me is a blessing I cherish. Help us to thrive as we serve You. In Jesus' name, amen.

February 3

Arm Yourself, Stay Alert

Pray in the Spirit on all occasions with all kinds of prayers and requests. . . . Be alert and always keep on praying for all the Lord's people (Ephesians 6:18).

Scripture: Ephesians 6:10-18
Song: "Put on the Full Armor of God"

For motorcycle enthusiasts, enjoying a leisurely ride is relaxing but can also be quite dangerous. Therefore, riders must remain alert. Animals in the road, highway debris, and inattentive drivers are life-threatening, and there's no telling what's around the next curve. Some bikers refer to these dangers as "road gremlins" and tie a "guardian bell" to their bike to fend them off. Lore has it that the bell's jingle brings gremlins to ruin. Although details of the legend vary, one constant is the tradition that a rider cannot buy his or her own guardian bell; it must come as a gift from another rider.

The apostle Paul shared the gift of the gospel with many people. In today's passage he explained that the protective elements of faith are like a suit of armor covering the soul and securing endurance to face opposition, with the believer's trust in God growing stronger with each test of faith.

We are blessed to be covered head to toe with the full armor of God. No matter where our journey leads, we do not survive by luck or superstition. Instead, we're sustained by the goodness of our Heavenly Father. His love surpasses all understanding and is the ultimate protection from evil along life's road.

Father, thank You that in Your wisdom and love, You've provided spiritual armor for me to put on each day. In Jesus' name, amen.

February 4

Enduring Patience

The Lord is the everlasting God. . . . He will not grow tired or weary, and his understanding no one can fathom (Isaiah 40:28).

Scripture: Isaiah 40:12-13, 25-31
Song: "Sweet Will of God"

Mothers of strong-willed little ones can tell some interesting stories. My son has the stubbornness of a mule and the drive of a wild rhinoceros! Unloading groceries is a weekly test of his physical strength as he challenges himself to pick up the heaviest items. He mastered milk jugs and has moved on to massive bags of dog food and great big watermelons! One day, he decided to grab a gigantic case of water. I told him it was too heavy, but unfazed, he somehow managed to pull it from the truck. As it began to fall, I caught the bottom, and together we carried it inside. Once there, he turned to show me his little muscles, thinking he carried it all by himself. Although his stubbornness is frustrating, moments like these are rewarding.

In today's passage, God provides consistent reassurance that He is patient. He doesn't give up on us when, at times, we try to accomplish our own goals without waiting for Him. He understands the determination of our human nature and doesn't grow weary of teaching and guiding us.

We often attempt to accomplish things or carry emotional burdens without God's assistance. Time and again, He catches us, and sometimes we may not even know it. Even when we're headstrong, He still loves us and cares for us.

Father, I'm grateful for Your patience with me as You teach me to trust and obey You. In Jesus' name, amen.

February 5

Dogs and Buzzers

As soon as they heard the sound of the horn, flute, zither, lyre, harp, and all kinds of music, all the nations and peoples of every language fell down and worshiped the image of gold (Daniel 3:7).

Scripture: Daniel 3:1-7
Song: "Oh, Be Careful"

Nobel Prize-winning Russian physiologist Ivan Pavlov (1849–1936) noticed the dogs in his laboratory drooling when the assistants came in. Pavlov surmised that the dogs associated the workers' lab coats with meals. He put this theory to the test and sounded a buzzer every time the dogs were fed. Over time the dogs salivated at the mere sound of the buzzer. This response became known as "conditioned reflexes."

Long before Pavlov's experiment, King Nebuchadnezzar applied his own conditioning to the people under his reign. Whenever they heard the king's orchestra playing, he wanted them to automatically bow down and worship the image he had set up.

God made us able to develop responses to the familiar in our lives. We can glorify God by establishing habits that usher us into worship of the one true God. When the snow falls, we can praise the Lord for His unique creation. When we see the flowers budding, we can rejoice at the newness of life. And the songs we choose to listen to can prompt thankfulness to our God.

Father, may what I hear, see, and do guide me to worship You and You alone. In Jesus' name, amen.

February 5–11. **Rachel Schmoyer** is a pastor's wife and a mom of four teenagers in the Lehigh Valley of Pennsylvania. She enjoys roaming cemeteries in search of local and genealogical history.

February 6

Who God Is

[Shadrach, Meshach, and Abednego said,] "If we are thrown into the blazing furnace, the God we serve is able to deliver us from it" (Daniel 3:17).

Scripture: Daniel 3:8-18
Song: "God Will Make a Way"

I flipped the calendar as I counted: only six weeks left on our townhome's lease. We desperately needed to find a new place to live. When I lay on my bed, staring at the ceiling, there was no comfort to be found in the uncertainty of the future. Instead, I recalled what God had done in my past, reminding myself that He is able to provide. A few weeks later, in a most unexpected way, God provided a home and the means to purchase it.

Facing a fiery punishment, Shadrach, Meshach, and Abednego had no idea what would happen next. However, they stood confident in their faith in God, knowing from personal experience what He was able to do. God had spared their lives when they were ripped from their homeland and taken to Babylon. God had given them favor in the eyes of the king's official when they asked for vegetables instead of eating the king's defiling food. And God gave them exceptional wisdom and knowledge as they studied for the king's service (Daniel 1).

In your times of uncertainty, remember who God is and what He has done in the past. It will help give you the faith you need in the present.

Father, thank You for who You are and how You have provided for me in the past. Help me to rest in You as I look at the uncertain future. In Jesus' name, amen.

February 7

Show and Tell

[Jesus said,] "Do not believe me unless I do the works of my Father. But if I do them, even though you do not believe me, believe the works, that you may know and understand that the Father is in me, and I in the Father" (John 10:37-38).

Scripture: John 10:24-38
Song: "Jesus, Son of God"

When I was preschool teacher, one of the highlights for me was seeing a child's face on show-and-tell day. I could tell whose turn it was because that child walked into the classroom with an extra skip in their step, their large backpack bouncing, a grin from ear to ear. In some cases, the child had been telling their friends that they had a particular toy. Their friends may not have been convinced, but show-and-tell day was a chance for the child to prove ownership of that exciting toy.

The religious leaders who opposed Jesus were disbelieving of His claims. Jesus drew their attention to what He had been showing them. The miracles—the good works that Jesus was doing—demonstrated that He is the Messiah, that He and the Father are one. He turned water to wine, walked on water, fed 5,000 people, and healed a man born blind. These good works proved that Jesus was who He said He was.

When your faith in God is tested because a truth in God's Word seems unbelievable, remember not only what Jesus said but also what He did during His time on earth.

Father, thank You for the testifying works Jesus did so we can know that You and He are one. In Jesus' name, amen.

February 8

Courage to Proclaim the Gospel

When [Israel's leaders] saw the courage of Peter and John and realized that they were unschooled, ordinary men, they were astonished and they took note that these men had been with Jesus (Acts 4:13).

Scripture: Acts 4:7-20
Song: "Jesus Saves!"

Mary Slessor's (1848–1915) feet were tired from walking. The Old Town village in Nigeria couldn't be much further now. The dauntless missionary mopped the sweat off her brow and adjusted the toddler strapped on her back. Traveling to new places was hard work, but Mary was used to hard to work. (She had been working since she was a child in Scotland, laboring in factories instead of continuing her education.) At last, she arrived at the circle of huts whose inhabitants had never heard the gospel. She took a deep breath and summoned her courage. Despite her nervousness, she stepped into the clearing.

Peter and John were uneducated compared to the religious leaders of their day. In the leaders' experience, such boldness as the two disciples showed belonged to the educated. Although Peter and John were unschooled, they were courageous about sharing the truth of Jesus. It was obvious that their confidence came from being with Him.

Jesus Christ has commissioned His followers to take the gospel to every nation (Matthew 28:18-20). Our courage is not rooted in any human measure used to deem us worthy. The boldness we have comes from the power of the Holy Spirit.

Father, give me courage to share the love of Jesus. Let me not to be discouraged or feel inadequate but to rest in Your love and Your equipping power. In Jesus' name, amen.

February 9

Whose Name Is It, Anyway?

[The high priest said to the apostles,] "We gave you strict orders not to teach in this name" (Acts 5:28).

Scripture: Acts 5:17-29
Song: "What a Beautiful Name"

My husband, Tim Schmoyer, does not have a common name, so what are the chances that there would be two Tim Schmoyers in the same graduating class at Bible college? During the senior class ceremony, a professor announced that Tim Schmoyer had won an award. Neither Tim got up to receive the award; both thought the other had won. When sorting out the mix-up after the ceremony, they discovered that half the professors had nominated one Tim Schmoyer, and the other half had the other in mind! None of them had been specific about which Tim Schmoyer was which.

The Sadducees were a sect of religious leaders who taught about God but who did not believe in the resurrection of the dead. The apostles also taught people about God, but they told of Jesus' death, burial, and resurrection and of the gift of eternal life through faith in Him. The Sadducees knew this was different than their teaching and forbade the apostles from using Jesus' name.

Since so many religions use the word *god* when describing their beliefs, we as Christians can bring clarity to our message by being more specific. We believe in our Lord and Savior Jesus Christ. We believe Jesus is God, and we have the privilege of speaking His name when we share about our faith.

Father, please give me opportunities to share that my faith rests in Your Son, Jesus Christ. In Jesus' name, amen.

February 10

Reunion Time

[God said,] **"Bring my sons from afar and my daughters from the ends of the earth—everyone who is called by my name"** (Isaiah 43:6-7).

Scripture: Isaiah 43:1-7
Song: "When the Roll Is Called Up Yonder"

In 2009, nestled among the trees of Flat Top, West Virginia, the annual Lilly family reunion made its mark on the world. A total of 2,585 Lilly cousins attended the event, breaking the previous world record of 2,369 set in 1998 by the Busse family of Illinois. To surmount the 1998 record, Lilly cousins came from 30 states and from as far away as England and Germany.

In today's Bible passage, Isaiah the prophet communicates hope to God's scattered people. Isaiah reminds them that God has promised to gather them from among the nations and bring them back to himself again. The promises in these verses can also be seen as pointing to another gathering of God's people at the end of time when we will finally be safely home with our Lord and Savior Jesus Christ, celebrating with one another in His presence—an *eternal* family reunion!

When we are feeling lonely or dejected, we can gather with other believers here on earth in our local churches, in small groups, or even over a cup of coffee. The joy and the belonging that come from meeting together can encourage our hearts and give us a taste of what we have to look forward to for all eternity.

Father, thank You for the hope of our future gathering with You and with our brothers and sisters in Christ. In Jesus' name, amen.

February 11

Keep Walking

[King Nebuchadnezzar] said, "Look! I see four men walking around in the fire, unbound and unharmed, and the fourth looks like a son of the gods" (Daniel 3:25).

Scripture: Daniel 3:19-28
Song: "God Leads His Dear Children Along"

At age 19, Norman Croucher lost his legs when he fell down an embankment onto a railway line. Rather than becoming paralyzed by fear of a future without legs, he became the first person with artificial limbs to complete the trek from John o' Groats to Land's End—the full length of the island of Great Britain. He also climbed many large mountains, including the famous Matterhorn in the Alps. Norman Croucher just kept on walking, hiking, and climbing.

Shadrach, Meshach, and Abednego were bound and thrown into the fire. But while inside the furnace, they were set free by the one who looked to Nebuchadnezzar like "a son of the gods." The three men were not paralyzed by fear of their situation but were up and walking in the fire with the help God had sent. They did not seek a quick exit but patiently waited for God's timing for the trial to end.

Hard times can threaten to paralyze us with fear or discouragement. When we are stuck, not knowing what to do, God is there with us. Though He may not prevent all the hard times, He is walking with us in them, ready to lead us to freedom at just the right time.

Father, thank You for walking with me through hard times. Thank You for never leaving me or forsaking me. In Jesus' name, amen.

February 12

Decisions That Please God

The [Hebrew] midwives . . . feared God and did not do what the king of Egypt had told them to do (Exodus 1:17).

Scripture: Exodus 1:8-21
Song: "Where He Leads Me"

During World War II, after the bombing of Pearl Harbor, approximately 120,000 Japanese Americans were rounded up and sent to internment camps. Many were US citizens forced to leave their homes and livelihoods. For years, they were confined in remote camps surrounded by barbed wire and guard towers.

After hundreds of years in the land of Egypt, the Hebrew people began to be persecuted and mistreated. Pharaoh did not see or treat them as fellow humans made in the image of God. However, God had promised Abraham that his descendants would become a great nation, numerous as the stars in the sky and the sands on the seashore (Genesis 22:17). So, in spite of Pharaoh's abuse, the Hebrew population continued to grow. Desperate to curtail their numbers, Pharaoh ordered the Hebrew midwives to kill all newborn boys among their people. But the midwives made the decision to honor God and let the boys live.

The midwives' obedience was risky, but God rewarded their faith. Their names are recorded in Scripture, and God blessed them by giving them their own families. Today we can choose to honor God as they did, not fearing the outcome but trusting God in all circumstances.

Father, I will choose to honor You today, no matter the cost. In Jesus' name, amen.

February 12–18. **Denise Scott** lives in Wentzville, Missouri. She serves in a caregiving ministry, helping folks who are going through a difficult time.

February 13

What Kind of Follower Are You?

[The disciples said,] "Even the winds and the waves obey him!" (Matthew 8:27).

Scripture: Matthew 8:18-27
Song: "I've Anchored in Jesus"

I'm considering following some social media influencers I've discovered. There's a foodie who can teach me to cook, but there are no samples to taste. I can watch a fitness coach build muscle and work his core, all without breaking a sweat myself. And with my favorite camping influencers, there's no tent for me to buy. I can just watch the duo's adventure on a screen and then go sleep in my bed instead of a bag.

Like some internet surfers, there were followers of Jesus who were half-hearted in their desire to join Him in ministry. They expressed a desire to follow Him but really just wanted to maintain their status quo. Selflessness and sacrifice weren't their priorities. However, even though the 12 disciples got things wrong sometimes, they were truly committed to following Jesus. They were in the boat with Jesus when a storm hit. The danger was real (Luke 8:23), and they panicked. But when they heard Jesus speak and immediately calm the wind and waves, they were both terrified and amazed at His supernatural power. They knew He was the right leader to follow.

Just as the weather on the Sea of Galilee changed without warning, our life circumstances can change without notice. When storms crash into our lives, we know that Jesus is still the one we need to be following. He's not sleeping or uncaring. He's still in control.

Father, help me to follow You wholeheartedly. In Jesus' name, amen.

February 14

Clarification and Comfort

Jesus answered, "I am the way and the truth and the life. No one comes to the Father except through me" (John 14:6).

Scripture: John 14:1-11
Song: "God So Loved"

When a father in the military is deployed overseas, his young child struggles to understand what's happening. "Why does Daddy have to leave?" "Where is he going?" Even if the child is told that Daddy will be gone for a year, he or she doesn't really understand how long that is until a birthday and a Christmas have passed. The child feels sad and confused.

In today's passage, Jesus' disciples were feeling much the same way. In the previous chapter, they had received a trio of troubling disclosures from Jesus: (1) one of the disciples was going to betray Jesus (John 13:21); (2) Jesus would be with them only a little while longer (John 13:33); and (3) Peter was soon going to disown Jesus three times (John 13:38). We can tell from their questions that they needed clarification. It wouldn't be until after the events of Jesus' death, burial, and resurrection that they would understand Jesus' words, "I am the way" (John 14:6).

Jesus is, indeed, the way. If, like the disciples, you have questions and doubts, you can take them to Jesus. If you're tired of soldiering through life alone or have lost your way, you can come to Jesus. If you need comfort today, seek Jesus.

Father, I believe in Jesus. I believe He is my way to You, my way through this troubled world, and my way to Heaven. In Jesus' name, amen.

February 15

Responding to Jesus

Jesus answered [Pilate], "You would have no power over me if it were not given to you from above" (John 19:11).

Scripture: John 19:1-11
Song: "Softly and Tenderly"

When I met my future husband, he gave me a lot of eye contact. Over time, he made me feel special. But I'm not sure we would have fallen in love and married if I'd been withdrawn and given him the cold shoulder. Likewise, it's hard to have a relationship with Jesus without being responsive to Him.

In today's passage, we see how the soldiers responded to Jesus. Instead of believing that He was the King of kings, they mocked Him by making Him wear a crown of thorns and by hitting Him over the head with an imitation scepter. They stripped Him, slapped Him, and spat on Him (Matthew 27:27-30). Pilate's response to Jesus was to find Him innocent. Pilate tried washing his hands of Jesus' blood (Matthew 27:24). Then he ordered Jesus to be flogged. Although it looked as if Pilate was the one in power, Jesus said, "No one takes [my life] from me, but I lay it down of my own accord" (John 10:18).

Yet Pilate was accountable for his response to Jesus, just as each of us is accountable for our response to Him. Perhaps He wants you to confess a sin, accept forgiveness, or give forgiveness. Perhaps He is calling you to respond to Him in some other way.

Father, grant me courage and humility to respond to Jesus right now as He deserves, to honor Him as is fitting. In Jesus' name, amen.

February 16

Leading Well, Caring Well

Be shepherds of God's flock that is under your care . . . not because you must, but because you are willing (1 Peter 5:2).

Scripture: 1 Peter 5
Song: "Gentle Shepherd"

Mary Teresa Bojaxhiu (1910–1997) was small in stature but tenacious in service. Known to most as Mother Teresa, she was credited with helping the poor, sick, and dying in India and around the world. In her lifetime, she received many honors, including the Nobel Peace Prize and the Presidential Medal of Freedom.

The author of today's passage had credentials of his own. Peter was leader of the early church and an apostle, an eyewitness to Jesus' earthly ministry. Peter encouraged church leaders to serve willingly and humbly, following the example of the chief shepherd, Jesus. Church leaders could be sure that God's grace and strength would sustain them even through hard times. A faithful shepherd must also tend to his own well-being by casting anxieties on Jesus and pursuing personal prayer, worship, and Bible study to maintain a thriving relationship with God. Leaders needed to resist temptation, setting God-honoring boundaries and fleeing enticements when necessary.

Peter's instruction for church overseers provides guidance for all Christians who lead, whether for a parent, Bible study facilitator, teacher, or coach. Faithful leaders can be sure that their labor is not in vain (1 Corinthians 15:58) and that they will be rewarded for their work (Revelation 22:12). Peter's most important credential was the same as for all believers: being united with Christ.

Father, help me faithfully lead and nurture those You've assigned to my care. In Jesus' name, amen.

February 17

Trust Builder

[Daniel] was trustworthy and neither corrupt nor negligent (Daniel 6:4).

Scripture: Daniel 6:1-15
Song: "Be Thou My Vision"

If you have a U.S. $1 bill on hand, you'll find the words "In God We Trust" printed on the back. Odds are, however, that you won't find a U.S. 1864 two-cent coin in your pocket. It was the first coinage to carry the national motto. A government may print "In God We Trust" on its currency, but it can't imprint trust in God on people's hearts.

Daniel had learned to place his confidence in God. The chapter previous to this week's passage refers to Daniel's wisdom and ability to solve difficult problems. He was trustworthy and performed his work with excellence. Other government officials tried to dig up some dirt on Daniel but could find none, so they set a legal trap that landed him in a lions' den. But this was not Daniel's first test of faith. As a youth, when first brought to Babylon as an exile, he faced a number of serious challenges to his faith as he served in the court of King Nebuchadnezzar.

Though a captive, Daniel served in a position of influence, but he did not rely on that position nor on the king who placed him there. Daniel was bold enough to respectfully speak God's truth even to kings. Every time he trusted God, he experienced God's faithfulness. We, too, need to view our trials as opportunities to grow in trust. Like Daniel, we can know that whatever happens, God will be with us.

Father, help me to keep choosing You and Your ways. In Jesus' name, amen.

February 18

Prayer and Praise

[King Darius wrote,] "He [the God of Daniel] is the living God. . . . He rescues and he saves" (Daniel 6:26-27).

Scripture: Daniel 6:10-11, 14, 16, 19-23, 26-27
Song: "How Great Is Our God"

It's easier to talk to your father if you have a good relationship with him. You feel free to ask him for help, but your relationship is about more than just what he can provide—more than using his truck or borrowing his money. You value spending time with him. And because you respect and trust him, you find opportunities to say, "Thanks, Dad, I appreciate you!" Talking to God is like talking to a loving father.

Daniel prayed daily, not just during crises. Those who conspired against him found him guilty of giving thanks and asking God for help. Though he tried, King Darius couldn't save Daniel. It seemed as though his doom was sealed as tightly as the lions' den. But the next morning, Daniel shouted to the king that God, the creator of lions, had shut the mouths of the beasts and protected him. King Darius broke out into a decree of praise to God: "In every part of my kingdom people must fear and reverence the God of Daniel" (Daniel 6:26). God rescued His servant and revealed himself to an entire nation, beginning with its ruler.

Before bringing your requests to God today, consider beginning with praise, focusing on God and who the Bible says He is: for example, *God, You are kind, powerful, and forgiving.*

Father, I renew my commitment to daily prayer and giving thanks to You. In Jesus' name, amen.

February 19

Waiting or Fretting?

This is what the LORD says: "When seventy years are completed for Babylon, I will come to you and fulfill my good promise to bring you back to this place" (Jeremiah 29:10).

Scripture: Jeremiah 29:8-14
Song: "Wait on the Lord"

I love persimmons. The sweet, juicy fruit grew on wild trees near my childhood home, ripening in early autumn. The soft succulence was better than candy. I was so eager to enjoy the fruit that I sometimes sampled persimmons before they were ready. An unripe persimmon is bitter and very sour. My mouth still puckers when I recall my efforts to hurry the harvest.

Years later, I'm still not good at waiting, especially in my impatient prayer life. God's promise to Jeremiah reminds me to temper my anxious spirit. God's Word to the Jews heading into exile is a long-term assurance. Their promised homecoming wouldn't be fulfilled for 70 years! Many of the believers who received that prophecy died long before it came true.

God operates on His own timetable. The seasons of nature and the seasons of life unfold on God's schedule, not ours. God provides harvests, fulfills promises, establishes justice, and answers prayers, but we cannot hurry God's pace. God will not be rushed, so we must learn to wait on the Lord. If our choice is to live either by faith or frustration, let's choose faith!

Father, give me faith that You will always do what is right, and You will do it at the right time. In Jesus' name, amen.

February 12–18. **Michael Brewer** lives in Kentucky, where he spoils his granddaughters, preaches frequently, and teaches college courses in Christian theology.

February 20

A Friend in High Places

All things have been created through him and for him. He is before all things, and in him all things hold together (Colossians 1:16-17).

Scripture: Colossians 1:13-20
Song: "Let All Things Now Living"

My thoughts whirled as the Christian astronomer lectured on the size of the universe. Our sun is one star among hundreds of billions in the Milky Way galaxy, stars separated by trillions of miles. There are billions of other galaxies beyond our Milky Way, and those numbers only reflect what our telescopes can see. In short, God's creation is immense beyond human comprehension.

Even more staggering than these scientific calculations is the spiritual truth revealed in today's reading. Those numberless galaxies were created through Christ and for Christ. In God's Son, the whole universe is held together! The binding force of the creation is not gravity, but grace. From the lowliest sparrow to the most far-flung galaxy, Christ rules over all. My mind boggles and my heart throbs with praise at the inexpressible greatness of my Savior.

Yes, He is my Savior and the Redeemer of all who accept His grace. The one who shepherds the constellations is our Good Shepherd. The one who calls the stars by name has called us to be His children. The Son of God holds the universe in His nail-scarred, almighty hands. Those hands also hold each one who calls on His name. How could we be any safer or our salvation more secure?

Father, I thank You that no power in heaven or on earth can snatch me from the hand of my Savior. In Jesus' name, amen.

February 21

A Work in Progress

He who began a good work in you will carry it on to completion until the day of Christ Jesus (Philippians 1:6).

Scripture: Philippians 1:3-11
Song: "Take My Life, and Let It Be"

My life is littered with unfinished projects: the tin whistle I never learned to play, the neglected beginner piano book, a copy of *Moby Dick* permanently bookmarked at page 174. Don't even mention the fitness equipment in the basement. I'm good at starting things, not so good at following through.

What a comfort that God doesn't lose interest in, get distracted from, or abandon His plans for you and me. We will not end up gathering dust on a back shelf in God's workshop or, worse yet, be pitched into the scrap heap. As surely as God has begun a good work in us by the grace of Christ, He will certainly fulfill His purpose in us. Our creator is also our completer.

Spiritual progress in our lives sometimes feels like two steps forward and one step back. Even so, we need not doubt that God is at work in us, smoothing edges, teaching lessons, and shaping us into the likeness of Christ. God won't quit until we have become all that He intends. Since God refuses to give up on us, let's not give up on God. It will be worth it when we see His finished project!

Father, give me confidence that You will finish every good thing You have begun in me so that I may someday stand before You complete in Christ. In Jesus' name, amen.

Tending the Garden

The creation itself will be liberated from its bondage to decay and brought into the freedom and glory of the children of God (Romans 8:21).

Scripture: Romans 8:19-28
Song: "This Is My Father's World"

Bible study has complicated my grocery shopping. Now I choose to look for labels proclaiming "cruelty-free" and "certified humane." At the supermarket, I'm trying to take seriously what the Bible reveals about God's care for His creation (Deuteronomy 25:4; Psalm 104; Matthew 10:29).

Paul tells the Christians in Rome that God's great redemption involves not only the rescue of human beings but also the liberation of the whole creation. We have God's permission to use the world (Psalm 8), but surely that doesn't include abusing it or its creatures (Proverbs 12:10). Figuring out how to take better care of God's creation challenges me. I'm not ready to give up hamburgers, but I care about how animals are treated. I want to make personal choices that protect land and plant life. I wonder how I can help make the oceans healthier.

Learning to delight in God's handiwork is probably a step in the right direction. Maybe the real challenge is learning to love what God loves, not only our human neighbors but also cedar trees, lightning bugs, and those pesky moles in the yard. I'm talking about love that nurtures and heals. That kind of love is bound to make a better world for us and our grandchildren to the glory of God.

Father, the beauty of Your love is all around me. Give me eyes to cherish that beauty and a heart to share that love. In Jesus' name, amen.

February 23

An Unscheduled Appointment

In their hearts humans plan their course, but the LORD establishes their steps (Proverbs 16:9).

Scripture: Proverbs 16:1-9
Song: "Guide My Feet, Lord"

I had set aside a day for pastoral visits but without success. A nursing home resident was visiting his doctor. A patient was out of the room for tests. One woman was traveling, and another was quarantined. Tired and frustrated, I pushed on to one final hospital contact on my list. After hiking across the broiling parking lot, I discovered that the patient I had come to see had been released an hour earlier.

Feeling utterly defeated, I turned from the desk and spotted a familiar face across the lobby. She was the wife of a local minister. Her husband, a colleague I knew well, was in surgery. I could see she was alone and scared. When I offered to sit with her, she almost wept with relief. I stayed until her husband was stable.

That morning, I had made careful plans that came to nothing. But in the afternoon, God led me to the most important meeting of my day. Without my knowledge, God had brought me to the right place at the right time. I still make plans, but I'm more relaxed these days. When my schedule goes awry and I seem to be spinning my wheels, I take a deep breath and watch for whatever God might have in mind. I'm no longer surprised when God has a better plan than mine.

Father, I think I know where I'm going today, but if You have something better in mind, I'm ready! In Jesus' name, amen.

February 24

A Plywood God

[The wicked man] sacrifices to his net and burns incense to his dragnet (Habakkuk 1:16).

Scripture: Habakkuk 1:5-17
Song: "All Creatures of Our God and King"

In a museum exhibit of movie memorabilia, I spotted a golden idol. The prop was a relic from the 1956 film *The Ten Commandments*. One memorable scene in the movie depicts the Israelites dancing and worshipping before a golden calf made by Aaron. On screen, the idol is impressive. In person, it is disappointing, a shoddy plywood construction gilded with paint. Clearly, it was cobbled together to last only long enough for filming, a shabby image, hollow and rough-edged.

Old Testament writers often mocked the idols of other nations, and Habakkuk joins that chorus. He charges the Babylonians with worshipping their own fishing nets. Since the nets provided a livelihood, the fishermen offered sacrifices to their fishing gear. Such foolishness is not confined to ancient times. Things we are tempted to idolize are worthwhile in their own right—health, family, financial security, national pride—but a closer look reveals that these things cannot save us.

We can be thankful for our blessings, but we must remember that it is God who sends those blessings. We can be grateful for the creation, but only the Creator deserves our worship. In the end, false gods always fall short. Idols, no matter how cherished, will not sustain us through turmoil and sorrow. Only the one true God can sustain and save us. After the plywood has buckled and the nets have tangled, the living God remains.

Father, give me the wisdom to love You above every created thing. In Jesus' name, amen.

February 25

Let Your Light Shine

[God said,] "**The righteous person will live by his faithfulness**" (Habakkuk 2:4).

Scripture: Habakkuk 2:1-5
Song: "I'm Gonna Live So God Can Use Me"

After John Clifton failed to convince city leaders to install streetlights in colonial Philadelphia, he took matters into his own hands. He hung a bright lamp in front of his home. The light, situated at an intersection, drew considerable attention. Neighbors followed suit, hanging lamps outside their homes. Eventually, the city council was won over.

Clifton started with a belief (or faith)—the conviction that lights would benefit his city. Then that faith spilled over into action, what we might call faithfulness. To apply a popular expression, it was easy to "talk the talk" about streetlights. It took more effort to "walk the walk," to hang a lamp and lead by example. Habakkuk reminds us that God calls us to both a believing faith and a doing faith.

Faith within encourages us to live faithfully on the outside. In turn, that outward faithfulness brightens the world and points toward the Savior we serve. I find that to be a helpful way to think about my Christianity: inward faith that leads to outward faithfulness. I wear a small cross inside my shirt. When it falls into the open, someone will say, "Oh, you're a Christian!" That's fine with me, but I'm praying for the day someone will tell me, "I already knew you were a Christian. I can tell by the way you live."

Father, help me be faithful to You today in everything I say and everything I do. In Jesus' name, amen.

February 26

The Best News

What I received I passed on to you as of first importance: that Christ died for our sins according to the Scriptures, that he was buried, that he was raised on the third day (1 Corinthians 15:3-4).

Scripture: 1 Corinthians 15:1-11
Song: "Tell Others of Jesus"

During a visit to my daughter's house, I heard crying outside. I opened the back door just as my barefoot 3-year-old granddaughter, Leo, reached for the knob, tears streaking her face. At the same moment, an older neighbor girl pushed Leo aside to announce, "Leo hurt her foot. I just wanted to tell you that." And off she ran.

I've never understood the need some have to be the first to share a piece of news, but I do find it rewarding to offer information that someone needs to know, especially when it points them to resources that meet a need. Sometimes, though, I forget that the most important words I can share with anyone are these: "Jesus died for you."

Regardless of how interesting or helpful our conversations with others may be, the most important ones will have eternal impact. We're surrounded by people who've never heard about Jesus' birth, death, and resurrection and what that means for them personally. When we share that news, we're pointing people toward the one who can meet all their needs.

Father, help me stay alert and open to every opportunity to share the life-changing news of Your love and forgiveness. In Jesus' name, amen.

February 26–28. **Dianne Neal Matthews** lives in Tennessee with her husband. She enjoys traveling to visit children and grandchildren, cooking, DIY projects, and serving her local church.

February 27

Selective Memory

[Dathan and Abiram said to Moses,] "We will not come! Isn't it enough that you have brought us up out of a land flowing with milk and honey to kill us in the wilderness?" (Numbers 16:12-13).

Scripture: Numbers 16:12-13, 23-34
Song: "Count Your Blessings"

I frequently hear people talk wistfully about "the good old days" when life was simpler. They're often referring to a time period that includes my early childhood. Although I do understand what they mean, I can't help reminding them of some modern conveniences and benefits that were lacking at that time. It usually helps them reevaluate their longing.

During times of trial, hardship, or suffering, it's especially easy to fall into this kind of mindset. When we shift our focus away from God and become fixated on our present difficulties, the past may seem better than it actually was. We may become blind to what God is doing in our lives right now. Trust means clinging to what we know about God even when we go through tough times.

As time passes, it's easy to develop selective memory without realizing it. But we can have "elective memory" instead when we choose to focus on God's faithfulness and love. If we believe that His intentions toward us are good, then surely we believe that He will lead us through the wilderness in His time. And we can be assured that the destination will be worth the journey, despite any rough terrain along the way.

Father, help me to stay focused on the blessings in my life at this moment in time, resisting the temptation to compare to the past. In Jesus' name, amen.

February 28

Dragged to Safety

When [Lot] hesitated, the men grasped his hand and the hands of his wife and of his two daughters and led them safely out of the city, for the LORD was merciful to them (Genesis 19:16).

Scripture: Genesis 18:20-22; 19:1-5, 15-17, 22-25
Song: "God Leads Us Along"

A scene from a movie I watched years ago has stayed in my mind: two men restrain their friend from rushing into a building that's about to be destroyed by a bomb. In that critical moment, the man's frantic obsession with the lab that represents his life's work overcomes his sense of self-preservation; his friends have to drag him away. Later, the man starts thinking clearly and thanks them for keeping him safe in spite of himself.

Sometimes God restrains us or even pulls us away from what we're clinging to. While He has given us free will, He may choose to overrule our choices or desires. God can see the end results of our self-destructive habits, toxic relationships, or any idols that we've allowed to interfere in our relationship with Him.

God often allows us to experience the natural progression of our disobedience to help us mature spiritually. But there are times when He intervenes. Instead of grumbling about a change in our circumstances, we can learn to trust that He has a purpose in allowing it. Later on, we may come to understand that it was His way of showing mercy and keeping us safe in spite of ourselves.

Father, thank You for the times You have pulled me back from something that would have eventually hurt me or a loved one. In Jesus' name, amen.

February 29

Trusting Our Judge

When they hurled their insults at [Jesus], he did not retaliate; when he suffered, he made no threats. Instead, he entrusted himself to him who judges justly (1 Peter 2:23).

Scripture: 1 Peter 2:13-25
Song: "Do I Trust You?"

I regretted taking the time to read through a conversation on social media. Someone had shared an opinion on a current issue, hoping to prompt a well-thought-out, logical discussion. Instead, it resulted in an online brawl with insults, name calling, and accusations between acquaintances and strangers alike. The original topic abandoned, each rude comment triggered another one in response.

Rudeness and verbal attacks seem to be accepted forms of communication in our society. And this often escalates to a new level when it's aimed at our Christian faith. Jesus knows how it feels to be mocked, falsely accused, spit on, beaten, and crucified. Even though He was sinless and could have stopped His persecution at any moment, Jesus endured it. He knew that it all fit into God's plan of redeeming people from the penalty of sin.

False accusations, unjustified criticism, even persecution may come our way when we don't deserve it. We might never be vindicated during our lifetime. These situations may tempt us to lash out in retaliation or to quietly grow bitter and resentful. There is a third option. God has promised that one day He will reveal hidden things and right all wrongs. Until then, we can imitate Jesus and entrust ourselves to the true judge.

Father, when I'm unjustly criticized or insulted, help me not respond in kind, but with kindness. In Jesus' name, amen.

My Prayer Notes

My Prayer Notes